My dearest Rionnagh,
This is so you ALWAYS have one more excuse :)
With all my love,
Andrew x

WHY STEVE WAS LATE

101 EXCEPTIONAL EXCUSES FOR TERRIBLE TIMEKEEPING

Dave Skinner is a comedy writer, actor and comedian who has worked with, among others, Steve Coogan, Rob Brydon, Armando Iannucci, Reeves & Mortimer and Johnny Vegas.

Henry Paker is a stand-up comedian and cartoonist whose illustrations have appeared in *The Spectator*, *The Observer* and *Prospect*. He has also written for *Mock the Week* and *Eight Out of Ten Cats*.

WHY STEVE WAS LATE

101 EXCEPTIONAL EXCUSES FOR TERRIBLE TIMEKEEPING

DAVE SKINNER & HENRY PAKER

Atlantic Books
London

First published in hardback in Great Britain in 2009 by Atlantic Books, an imprint of Atlantic Books Ltd.

This paperback edition published in Great Britain in 2013 by Atlantic Books.

10 9 8 7 6 5 4 3 2 1

A CIP catalogue record for this book is available from the British Library.

Paperback ISBN: 978 178239 185 2

Printed in Italy by 🦓 Grafica Veneta SpA

Atlantic Books
An Imprint of Atlantic Books Ltd
Ormond House
26–27 Boswell Street
London
WC1N 3JZ

www.atlantic-books.co.uk

With thanks to:
Yakup and Ruth Paker,
Geoff and Inez Skinner,
Sally-Anne Johnson,
Sarah Norman, Camilla Hornby
all at Atlantic
and
Matt Peover and Tony Horspool

Meet Steve.

This year Steve was late 101 times.

These are the excuses he gave...

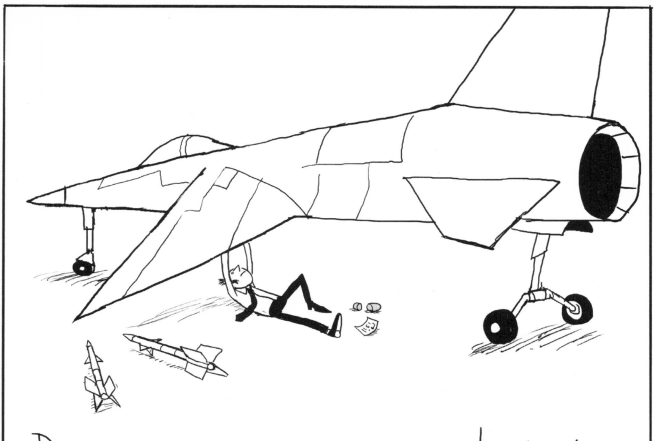

Distracted by a surprisingly complicated Kinder toy

1

Overcome by the urge to alphabetise my pets

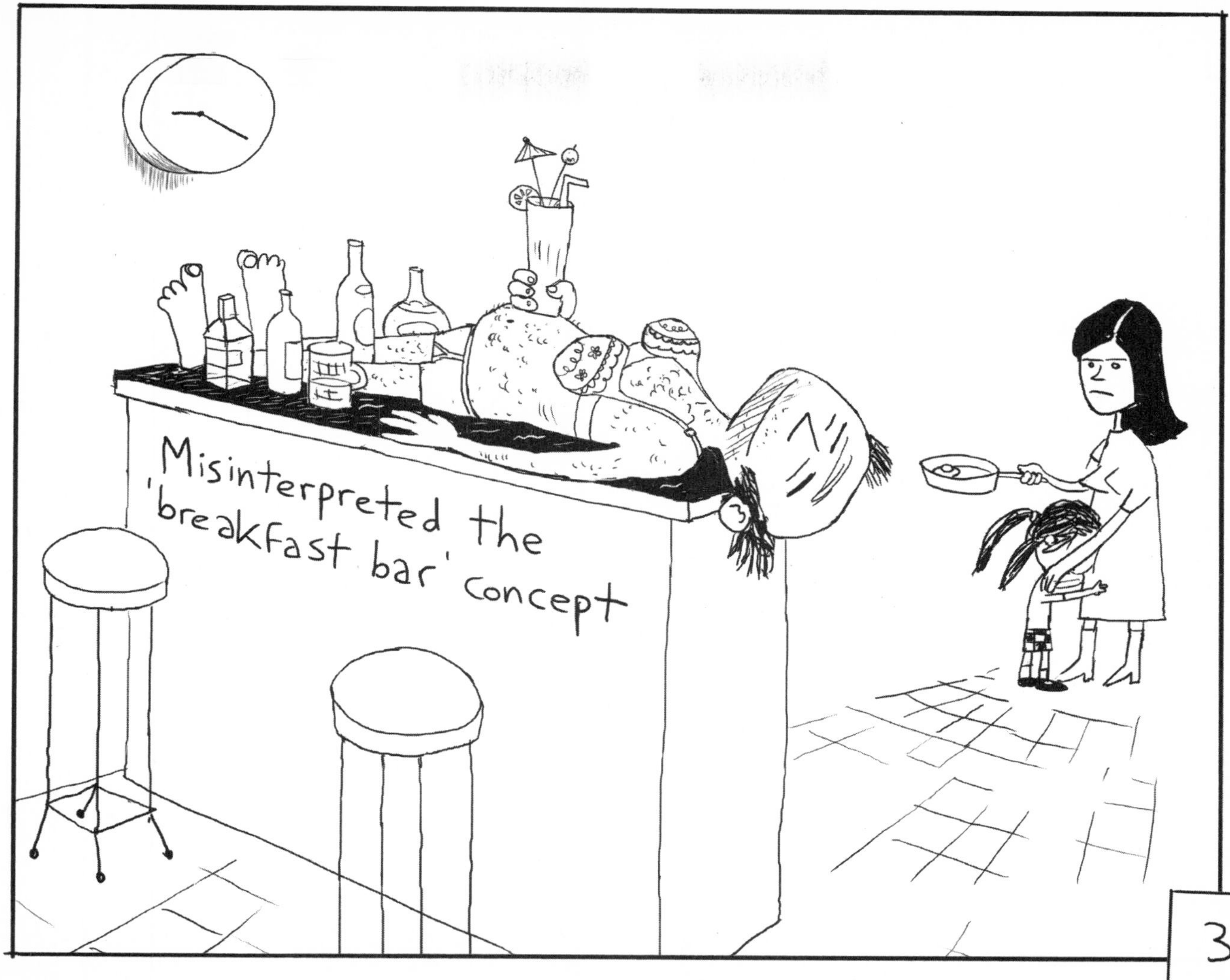
Misinterpreted the 'breakfast bar' concept

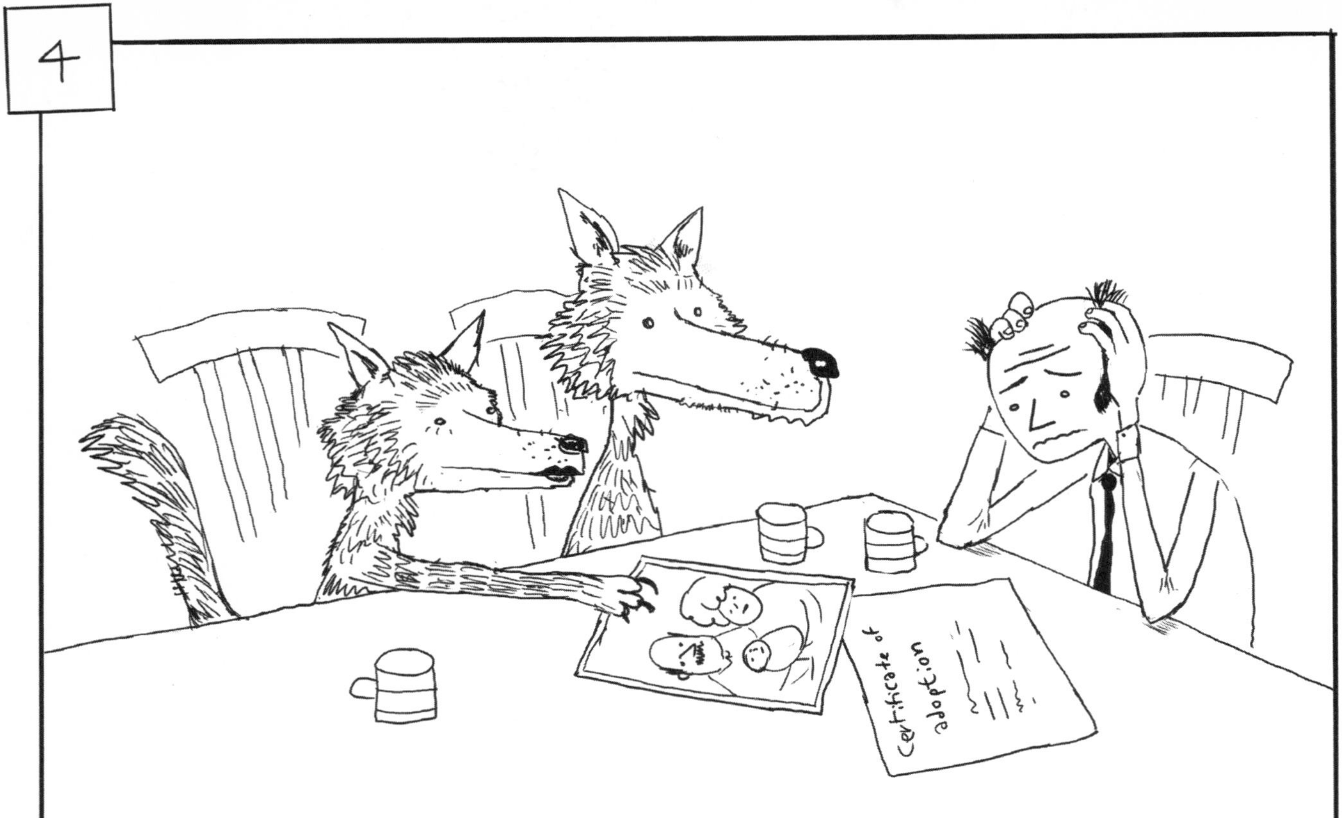
4
Certificate of adoption

Found out I'm adopted

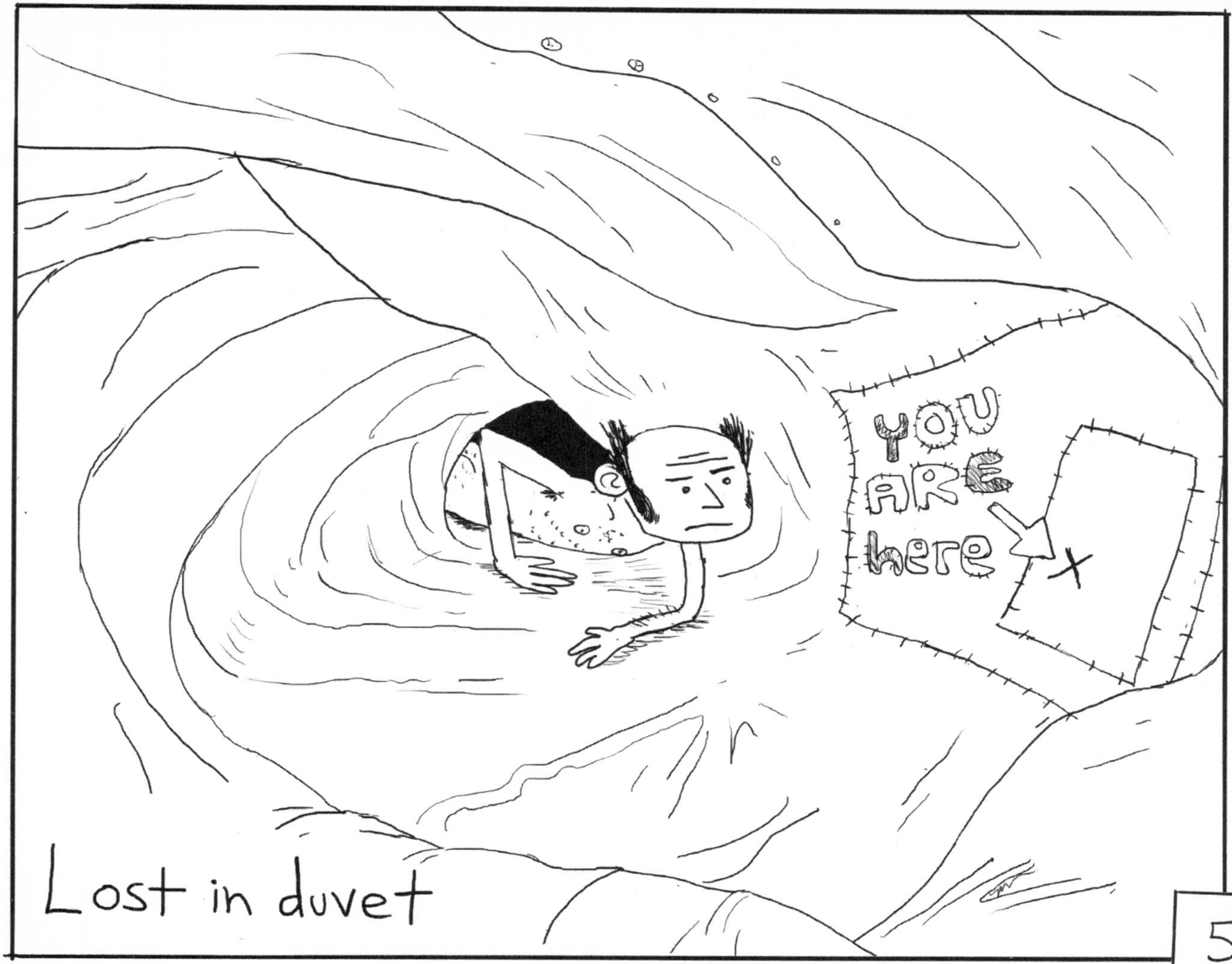
YOU ARE here
Lost in duvet

Distracted by world's biggest Sudoku

Forgot how trousers work

7

Accidentally sold myself on eBay

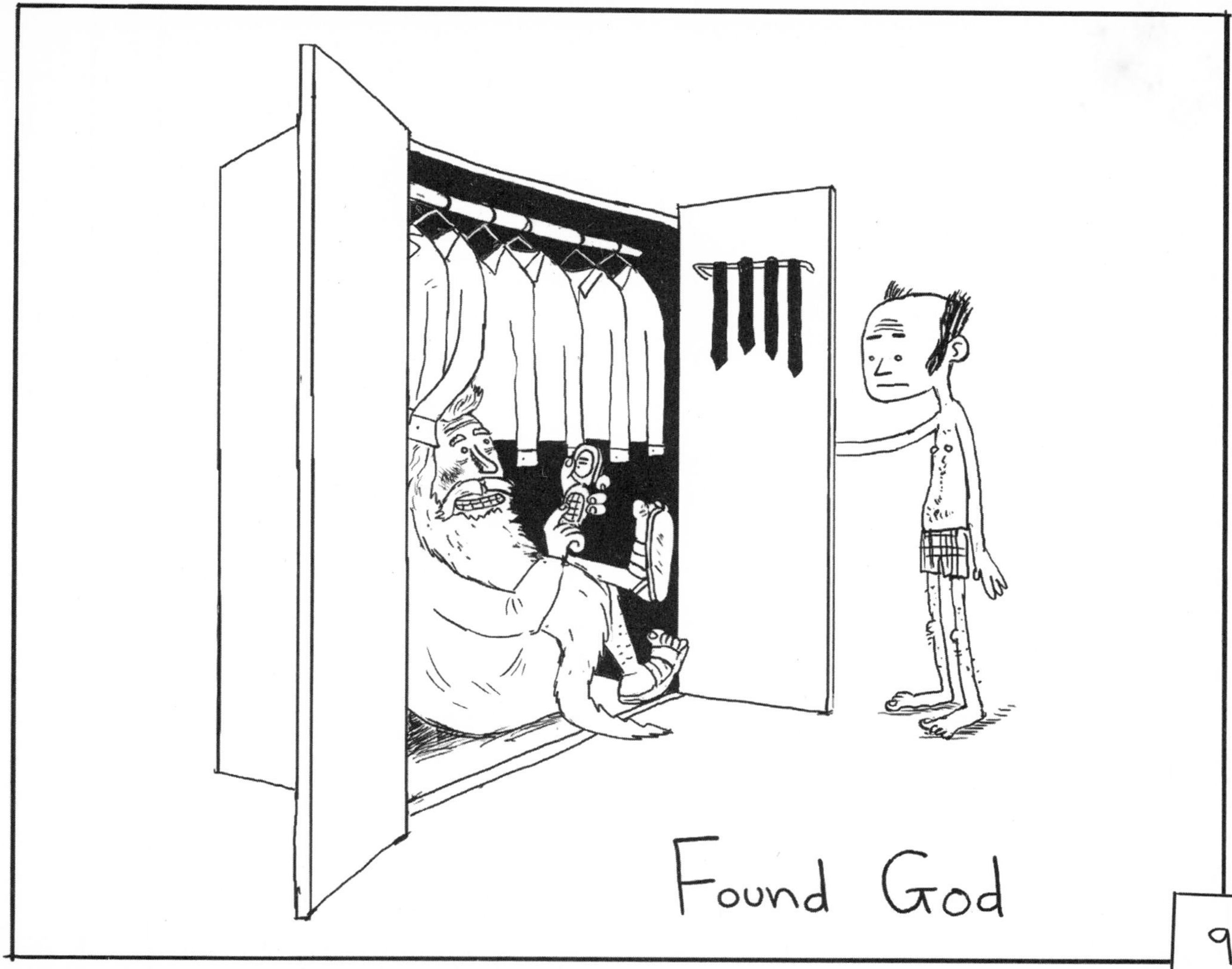
Found God

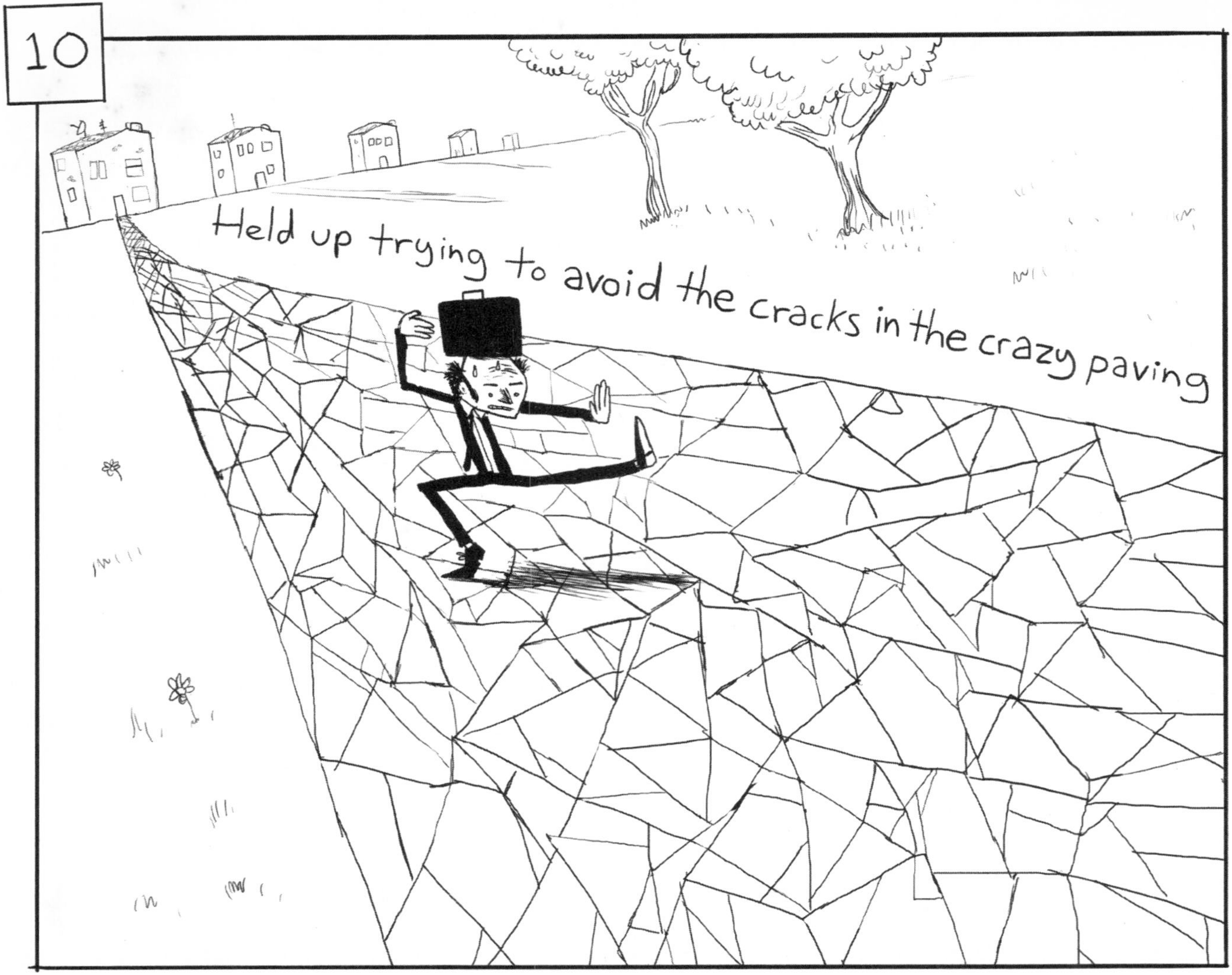
10
Held up trying to avoid the cracks in the crazy paving

Got stuck in a romantic montage

11

Overwhelmed by the breakfast buffet

Discovered I have an unusual superpower

Broke world record for longest ever awkward pause

Bumped into my arch nemesis

15

16

Family event dragged on

Marooned on a traffic island

17

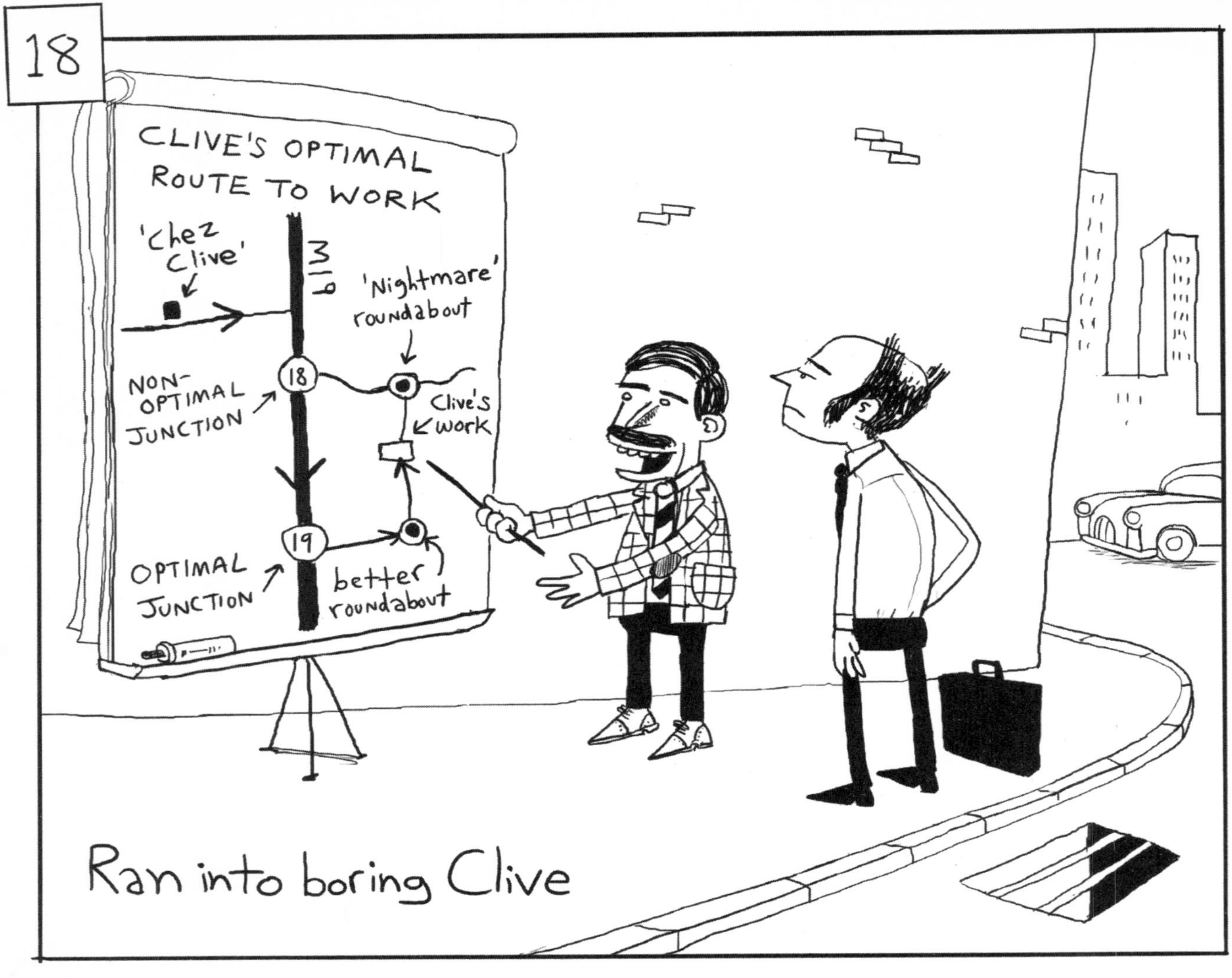
18
CLIVE'S OPTIMAL ROUTE TO WORK
'Chez Clive'
M19
'Nightmare' roundabout
18
NON-OPTIMAL JUNCTION
Clive's work
19
OPTIMAL JUNCTION
better roundabout
Ran into boring Clive

Discovered I'm jam intolerant

19

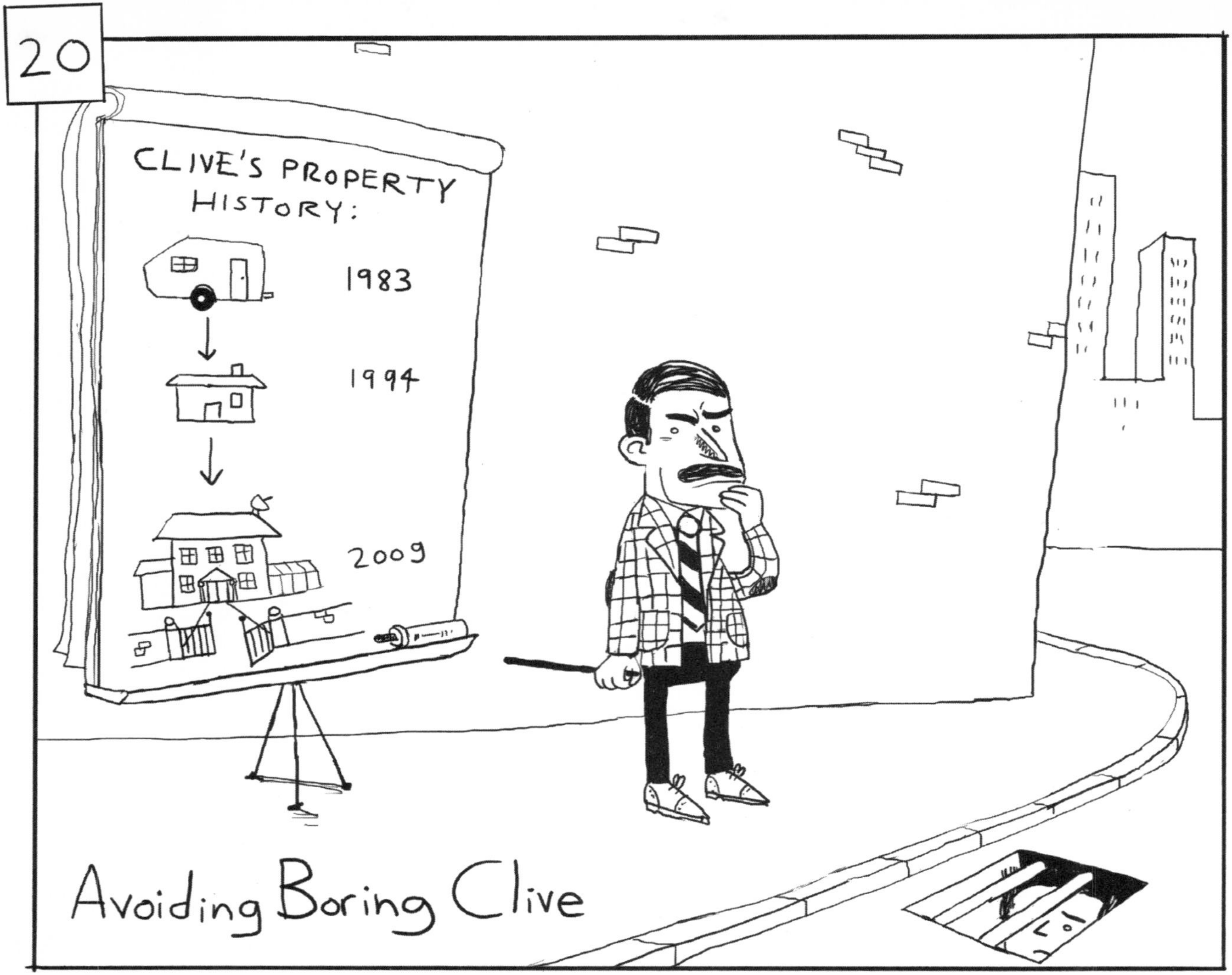
20
CLIVE'S PROPERTY HISTORY:
1983
1994
2009

Avoiding Boring Clive

Woke up with Magritte Syndrome

21

Turns out it's contagious

Involved in a vending mishap

PLATFORMS 6-11 →

Departures

23

Made an unpopular wallpaper choice

Fell in love with the voice in the Sat Nav

25

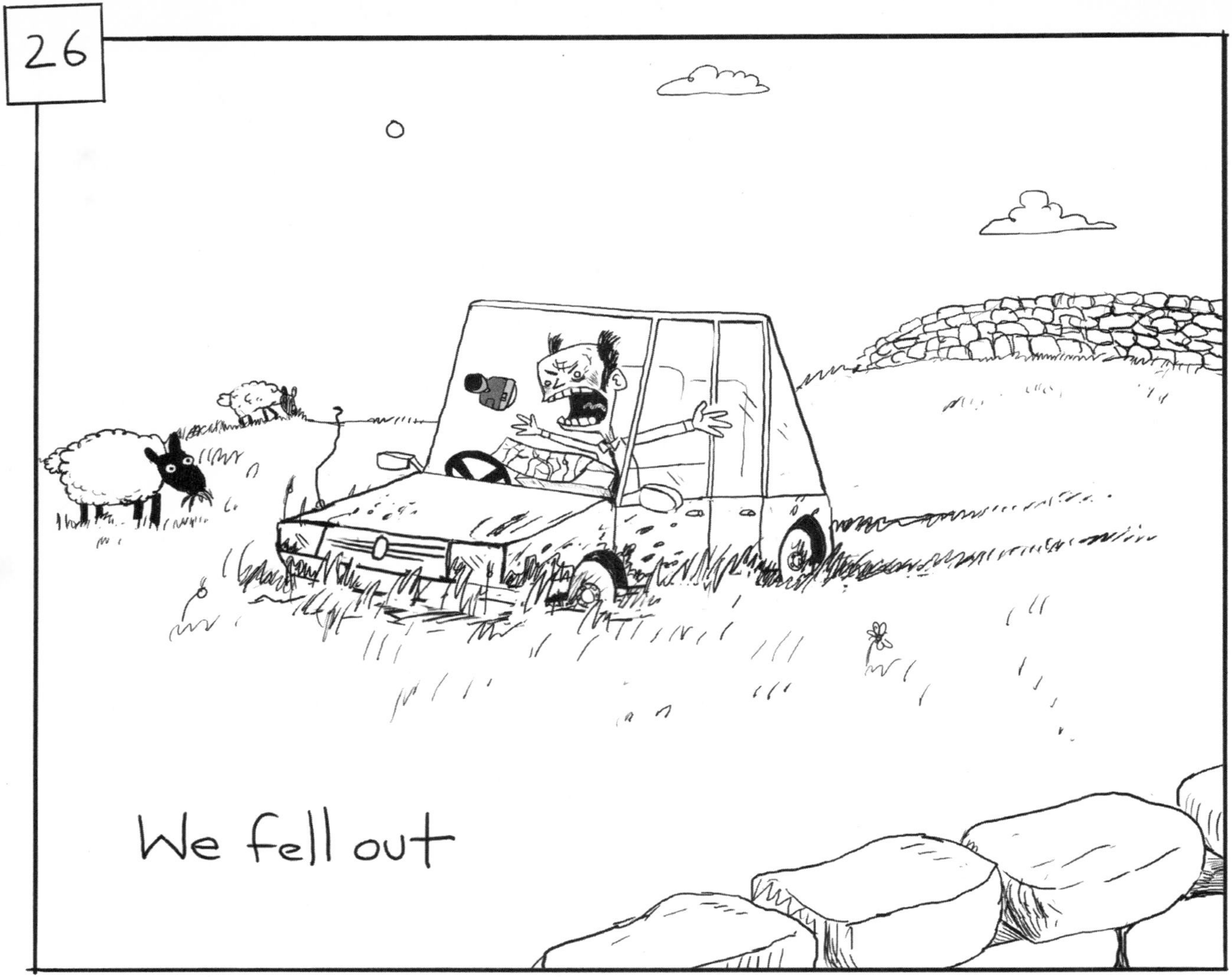
26
We fell out

Went to the wrong workplace

27

Couldn't decide which pen to wear

Got off at the wrong stop

29

Didn't know what to do with my hair

Went temporarily feral

31

Rubik's Cube took ages in a black and white world

Promised I'd take the kids to Hogwarts

33

Had a falling out with my neighbour

Having trouble with the builders

35

36

Shouldn't have skipped gym induction

Seduced by the Dark Side

37

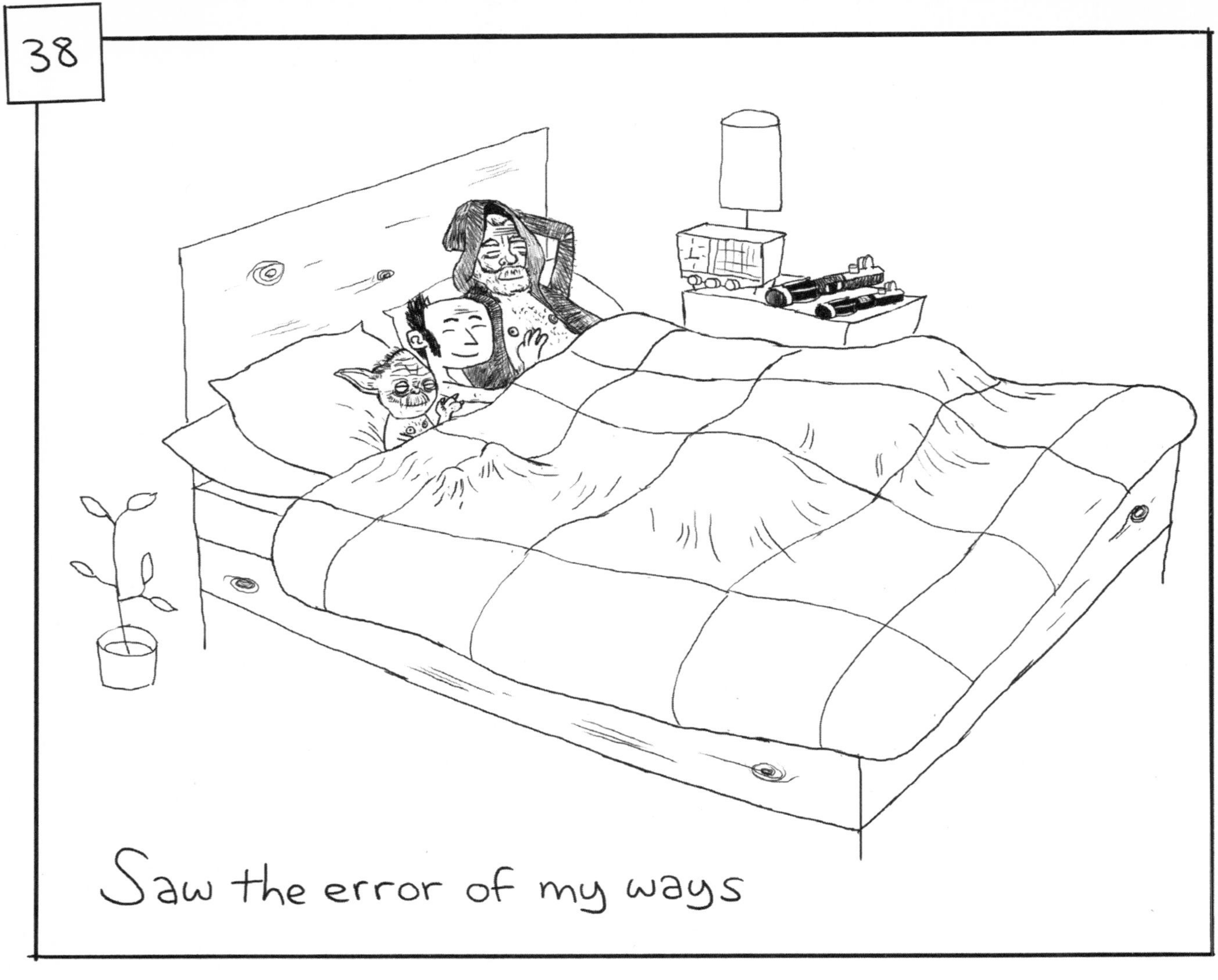
38
Saw the error of my ways

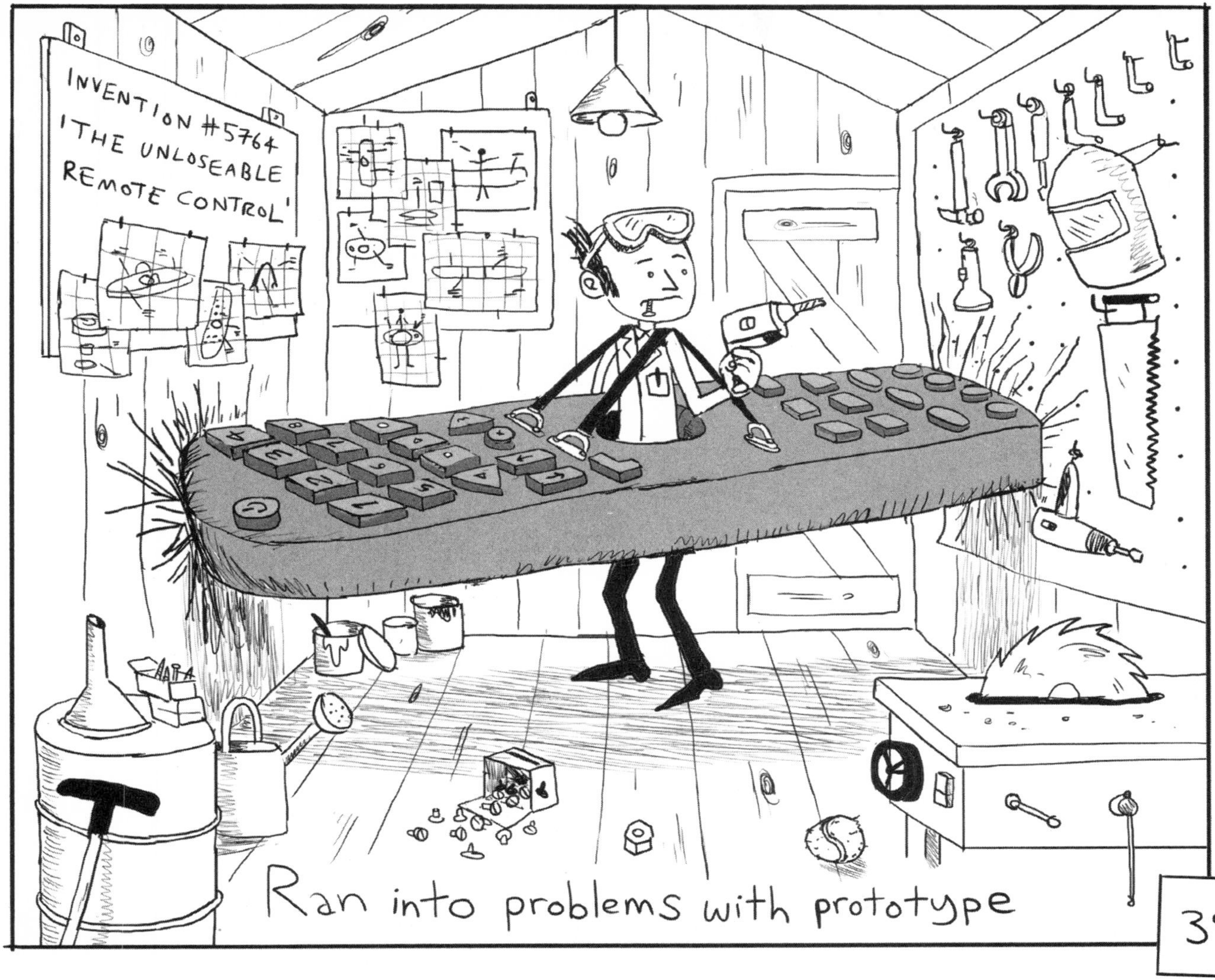
INVENTION #5764
'THE UNLOSEABLE REMOTE CONTROL'
Ran into problems with prototype

Competitive streak got out of hand

Mugged by mime artists

41

42

Dental hygienist was more thorough than usual

Had to attend a police line-up

43

44

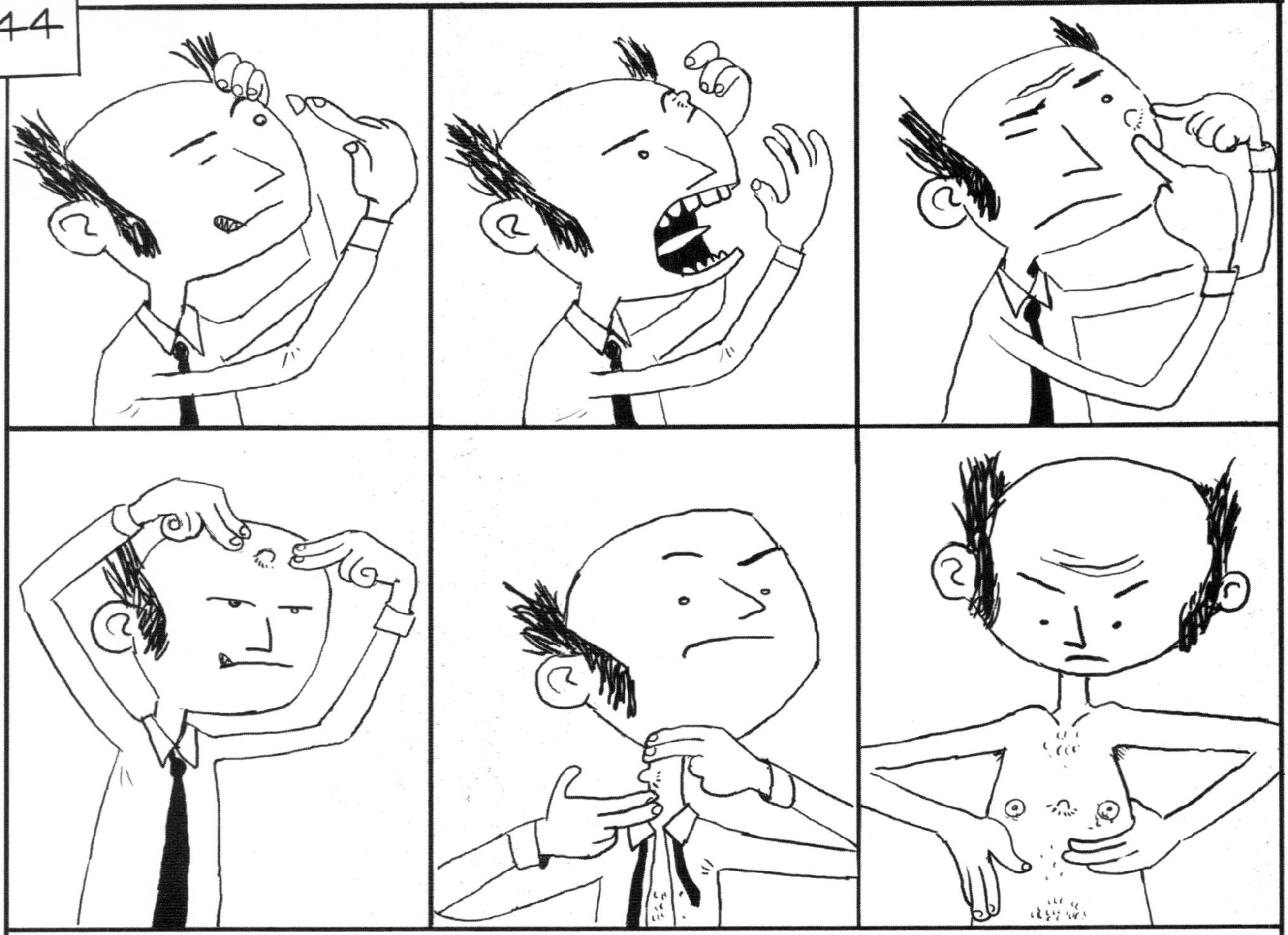

Lost a contact lens

Promised I'd wait in for neighbour's delivery

45

Birthday surprise backfired

Built a machine that turned against me

47

Had to win at Hide and Seek

Caught up in a breaking news story

49

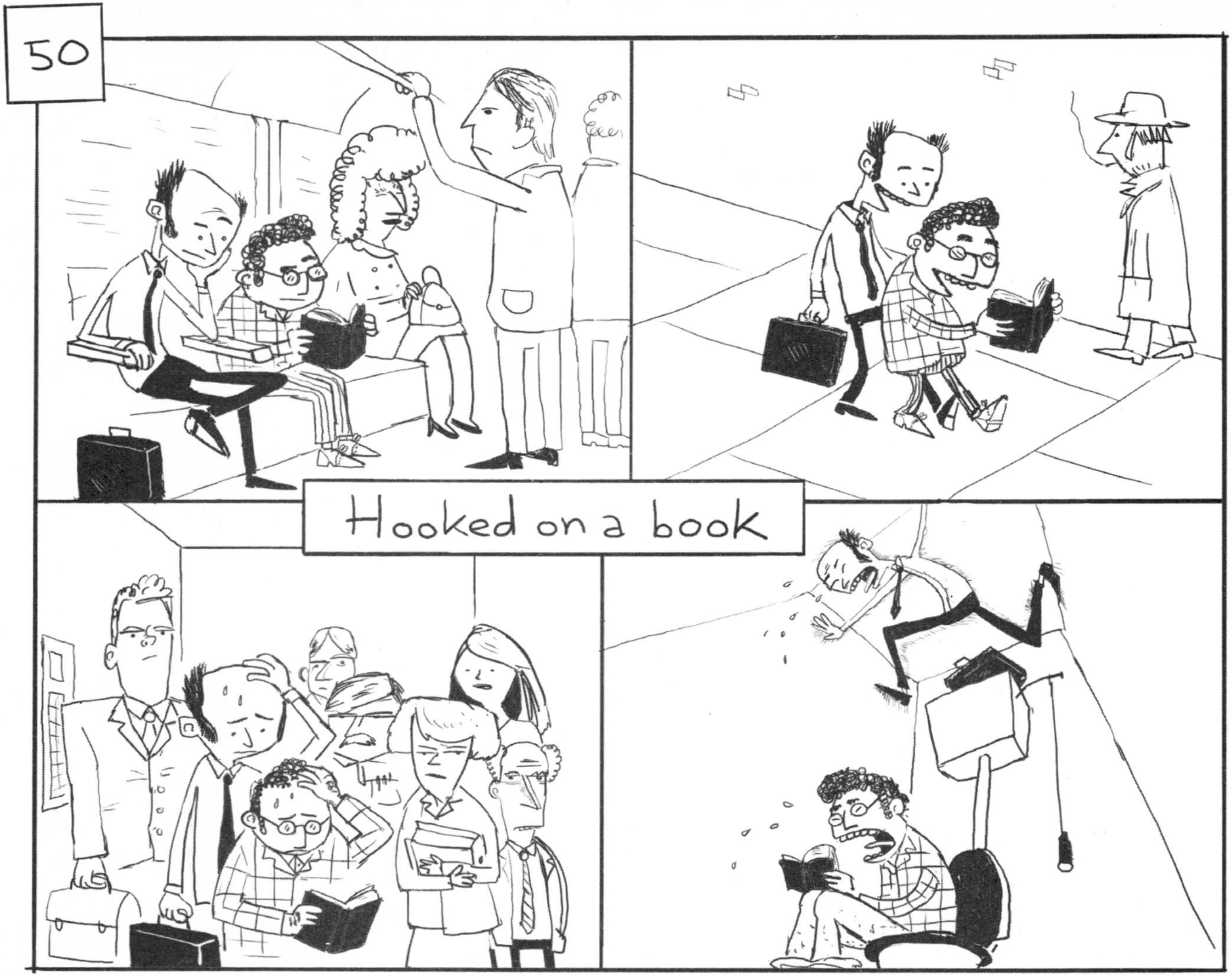
50
Hooked on a book

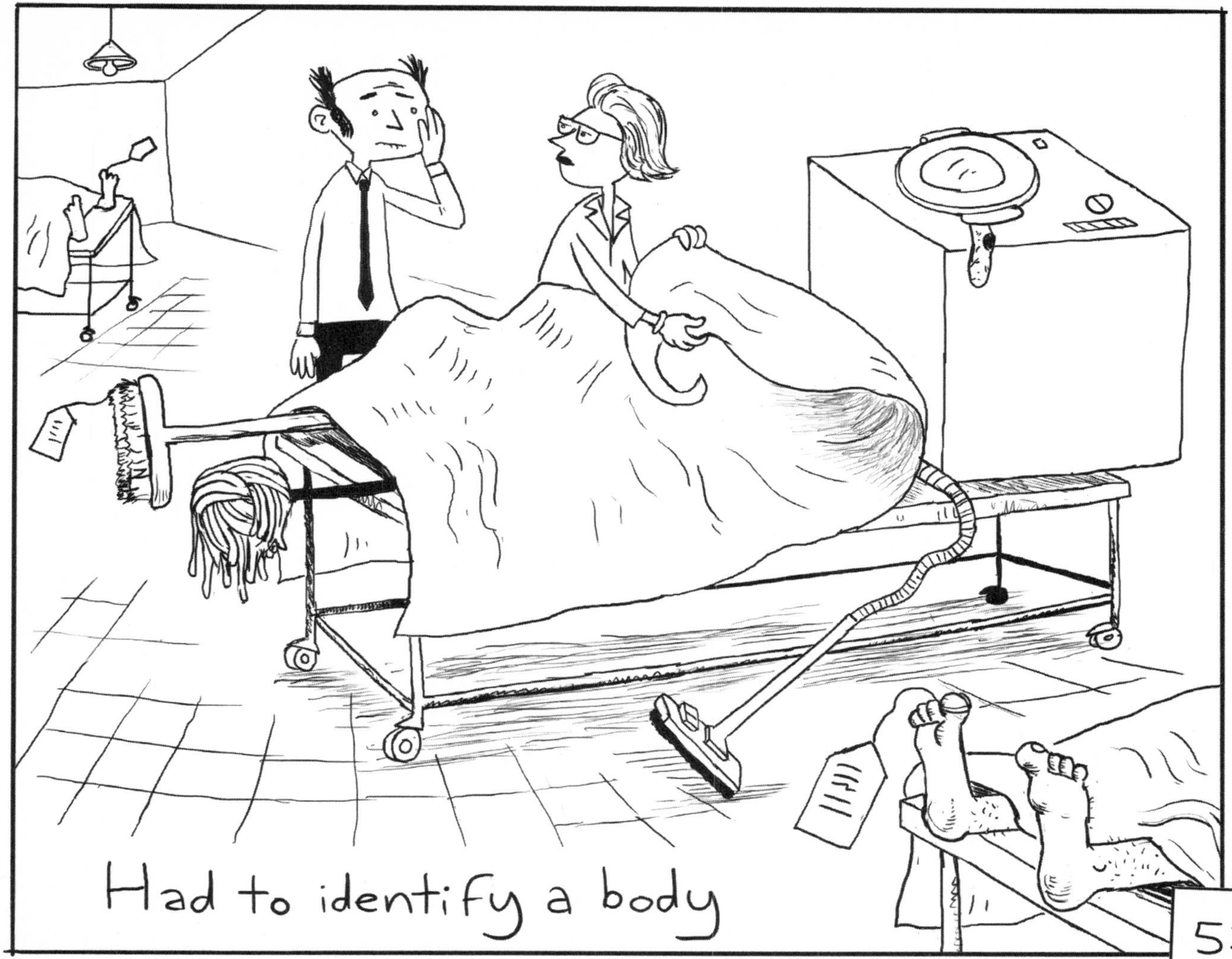
Had to identify a body

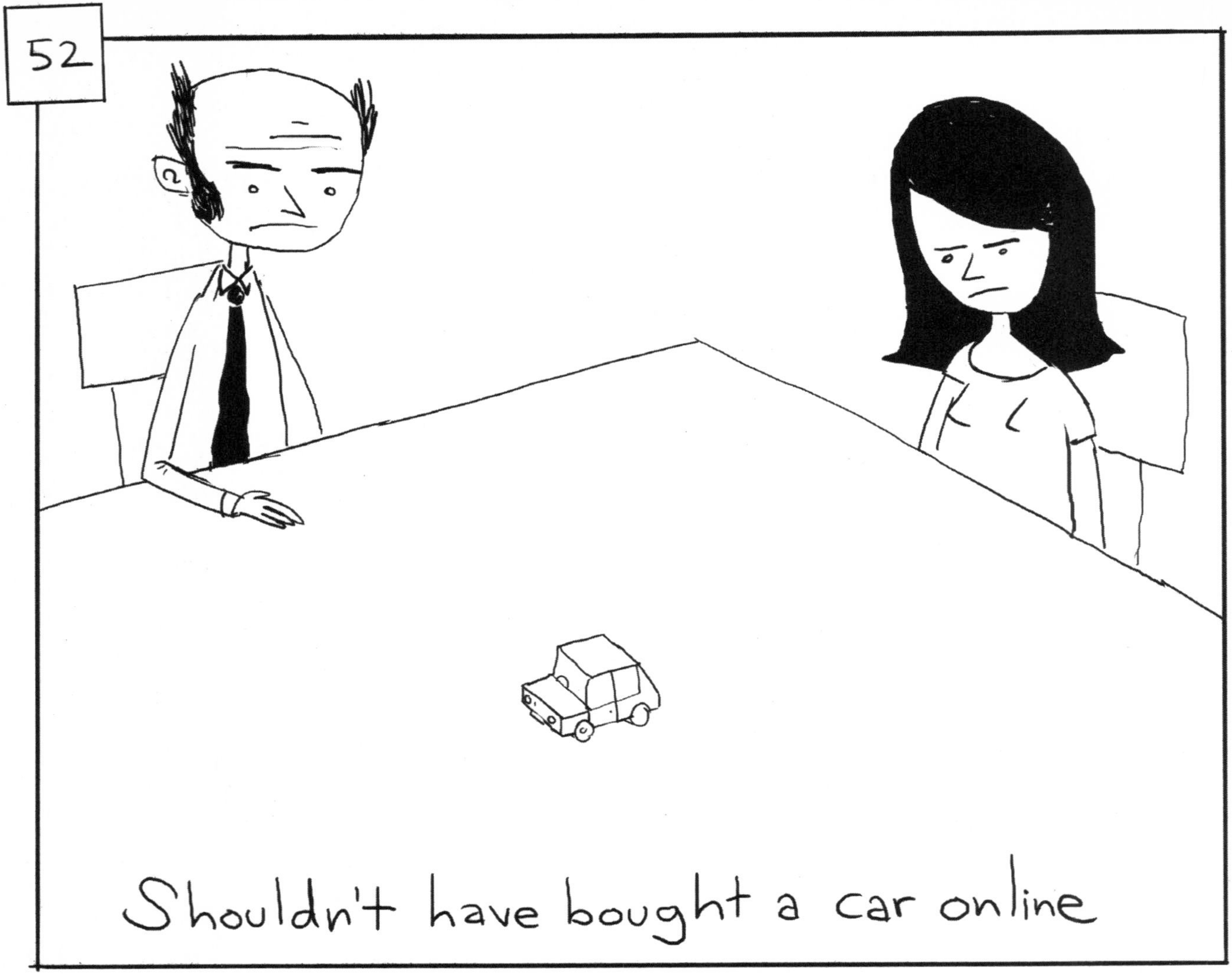
52

Shouldn't have bought a car online

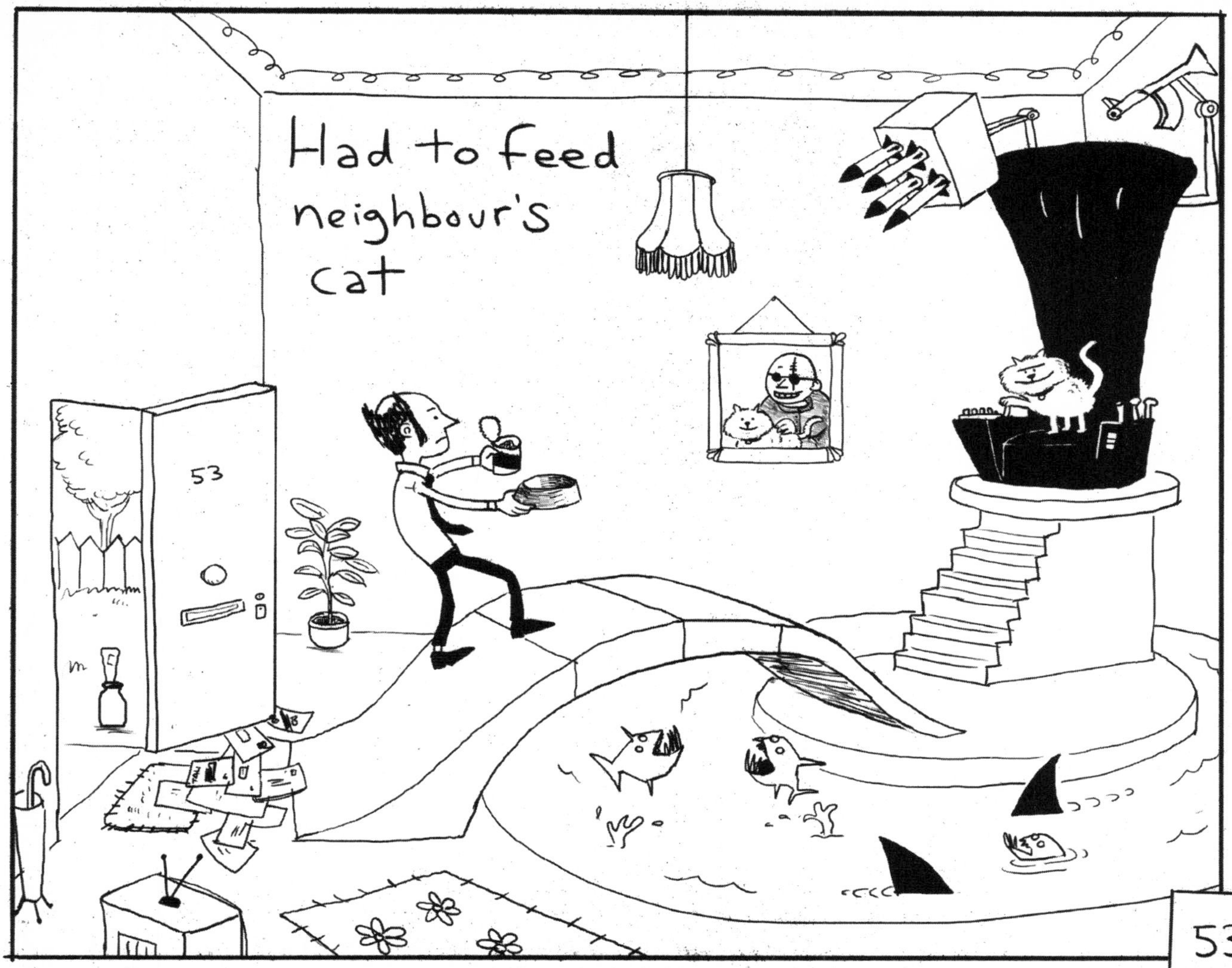
Had to feed neighbour's cat
53

Read something that upset me

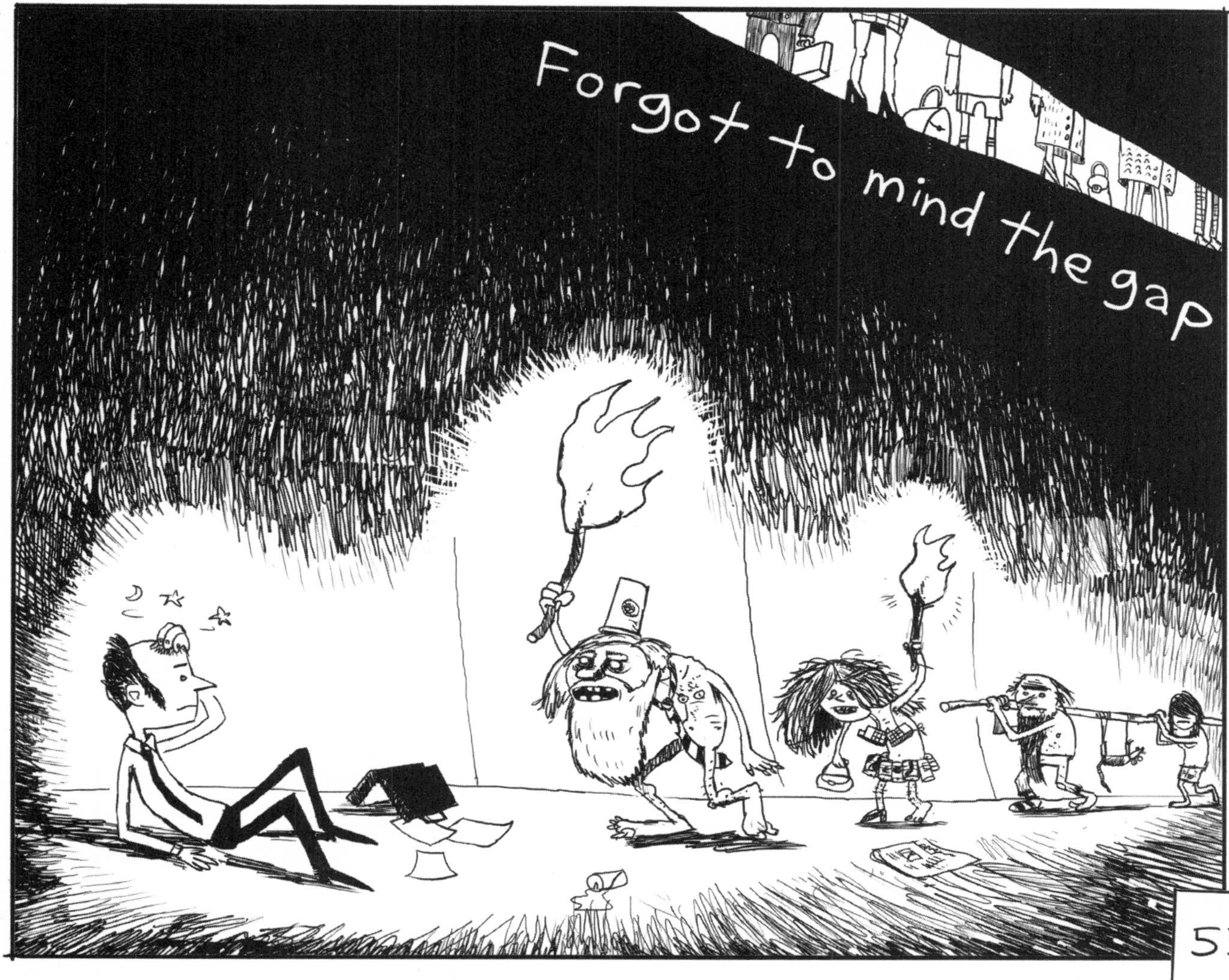
Forgot to mind the gap

56

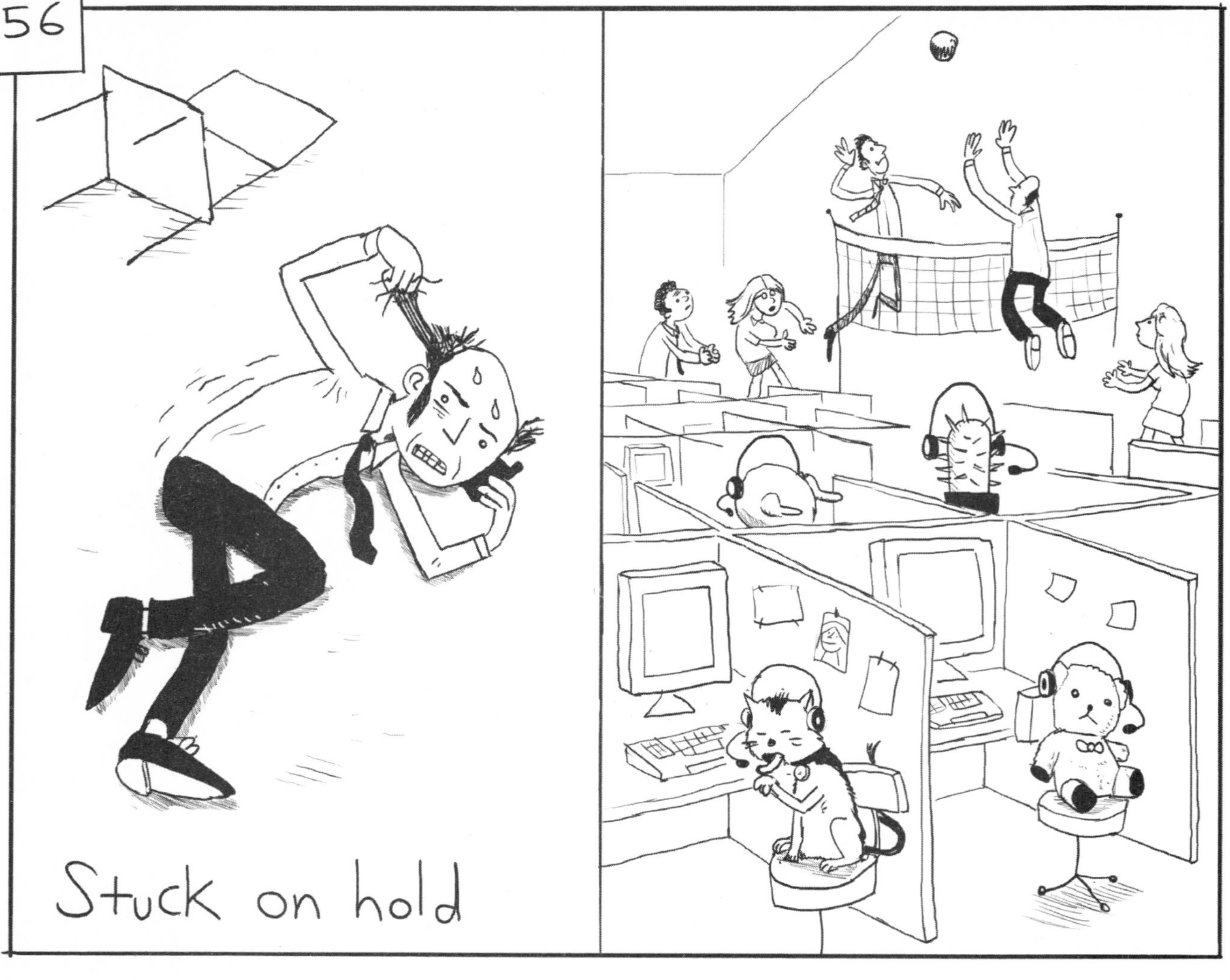
Stuck on hold

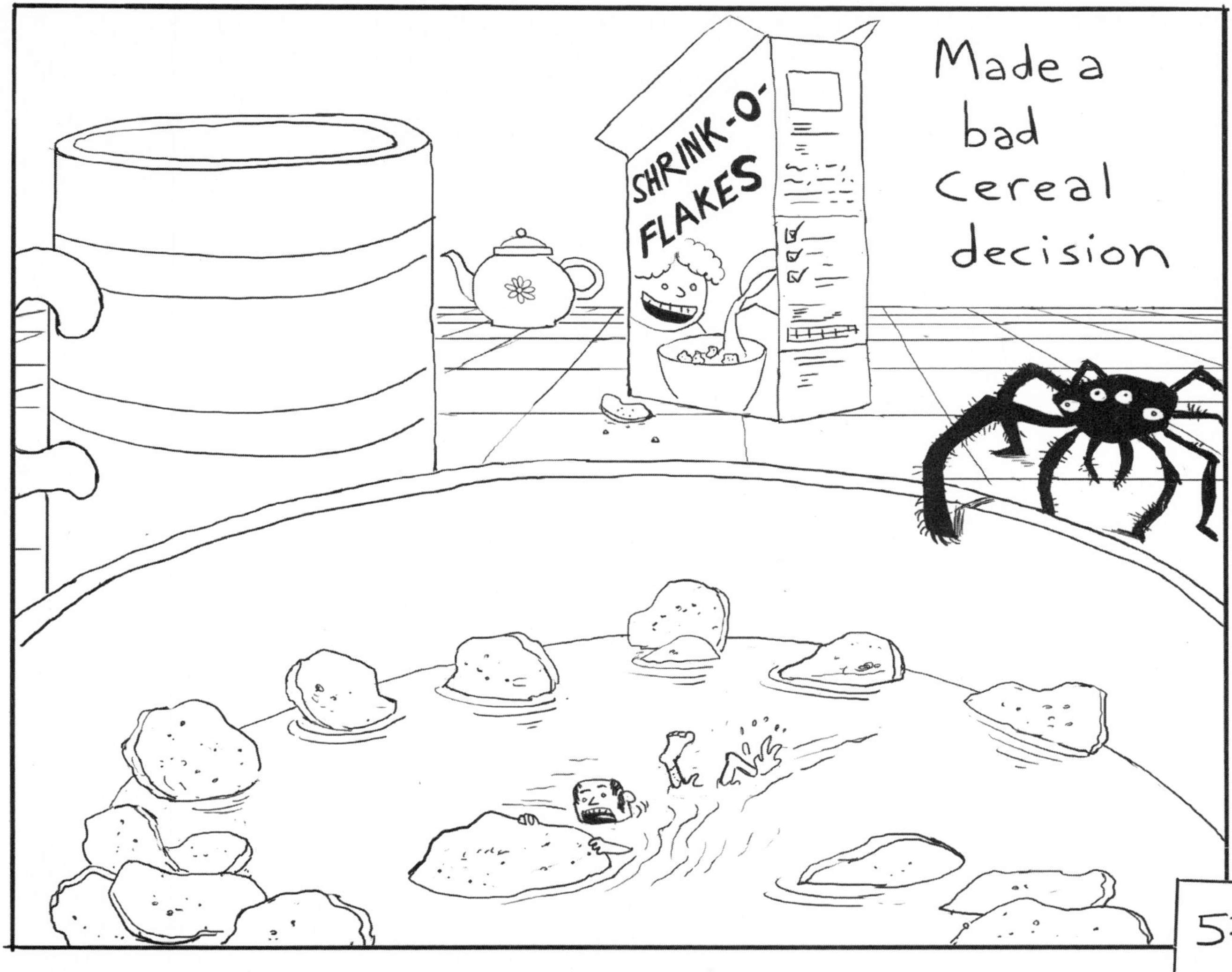
Made a bad Cereal decision
SHRINK-O-FLAKES

Determined to get the last out of the toothpaste

Flushed in a train station

59

Morning meditation went too well

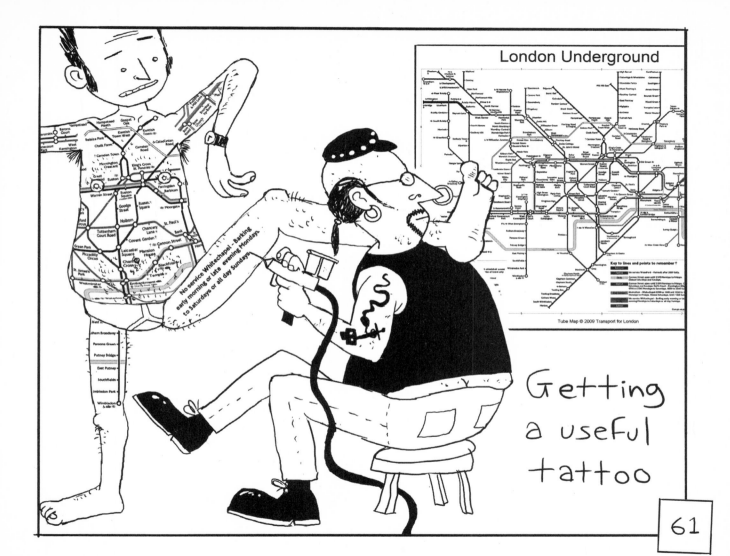

London Underground

Tube Map © 2009 Transport for London

Getting a useful tattoo

61

Held up giving directions

Getting to grips with my new phone

63

Testing my child for talent

Abducted by aliens

66

Abducted by other aliens

Subjected to a series of humiliating tests

67

68

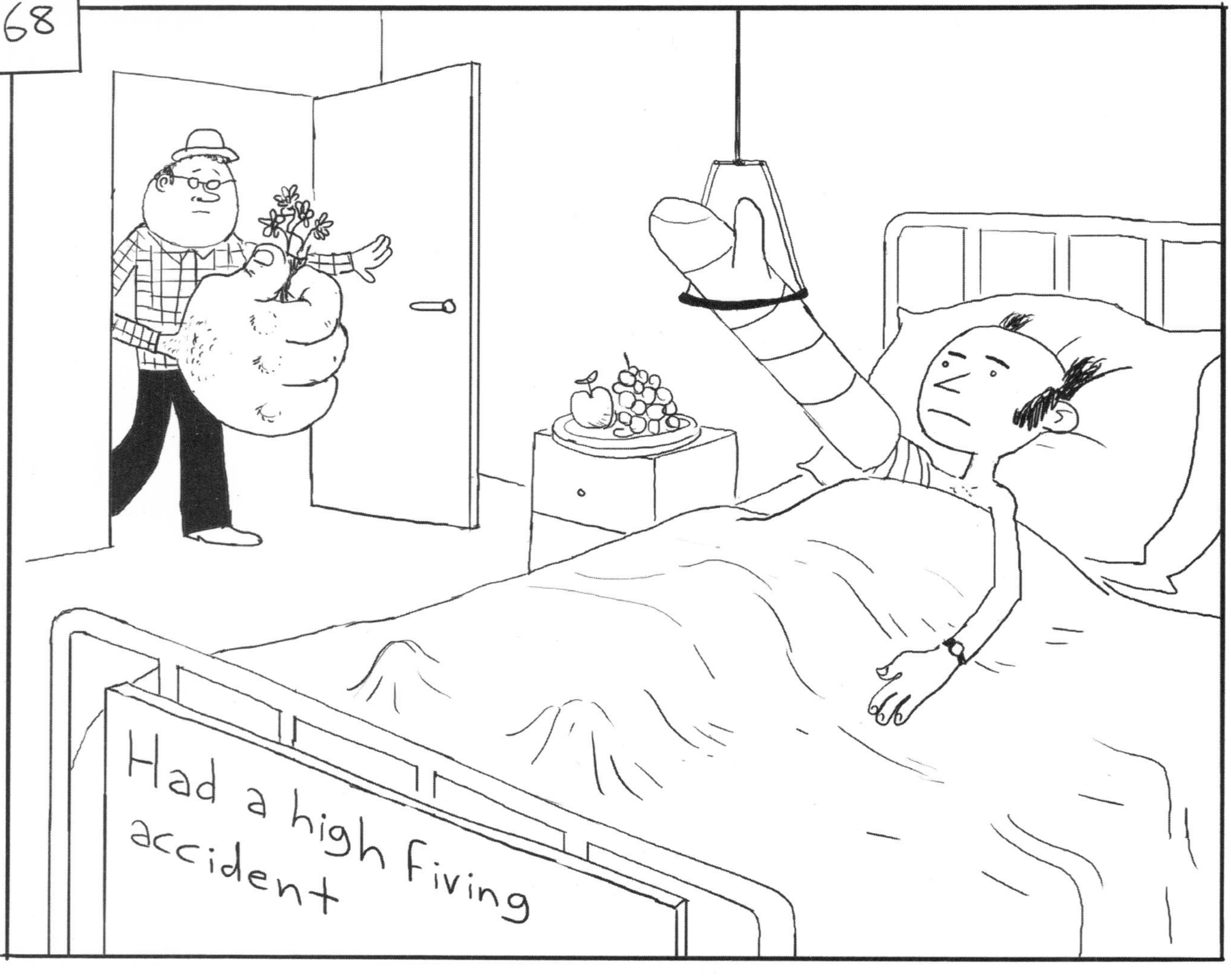
Had a high fiving
accident

My inner boy scout got the better of me

69

Last night's seafood came back to haunt me

Home hair transplant had unexpected side effects

71

Children possessed at breakfast

Attacked by brass rubbers

73

74

Got lost at a Where's Wally? Convention

Suffered a porridge catastrophe

75

76

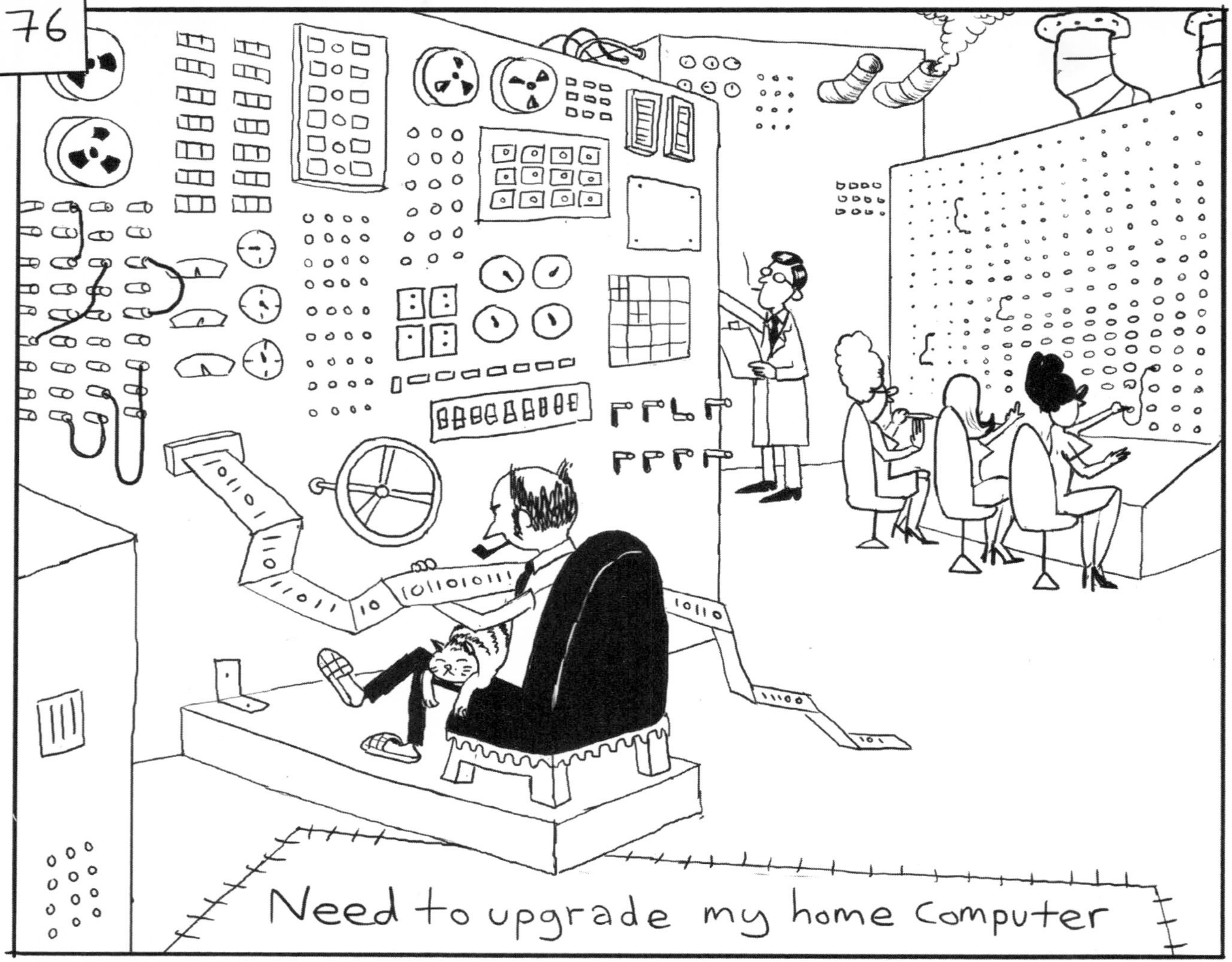

Need to upgrade my home computer

Became a YouTube phenomenon

77

78

A bad situation deteriorated

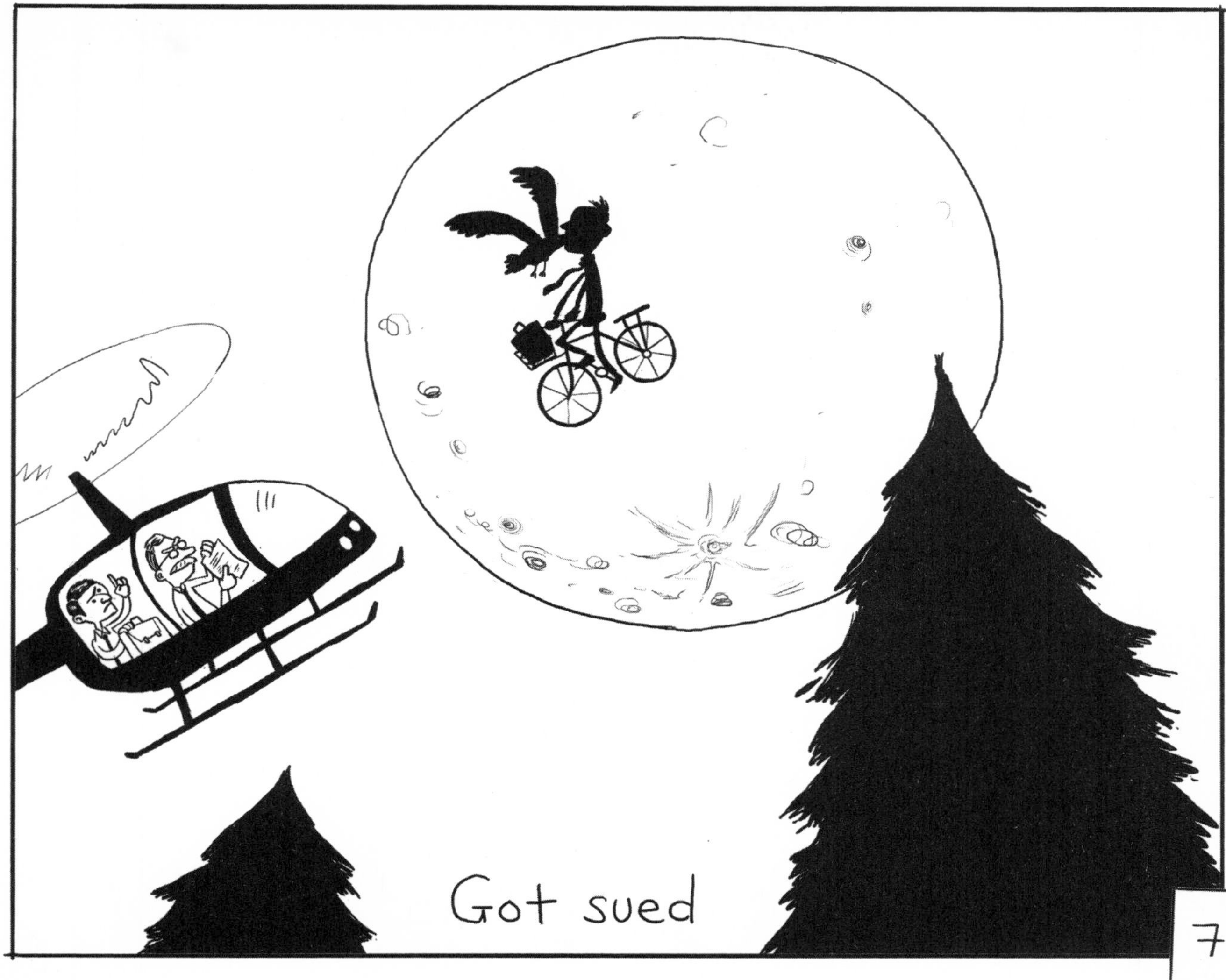
Got sued

79

Forgot to put away the crayons

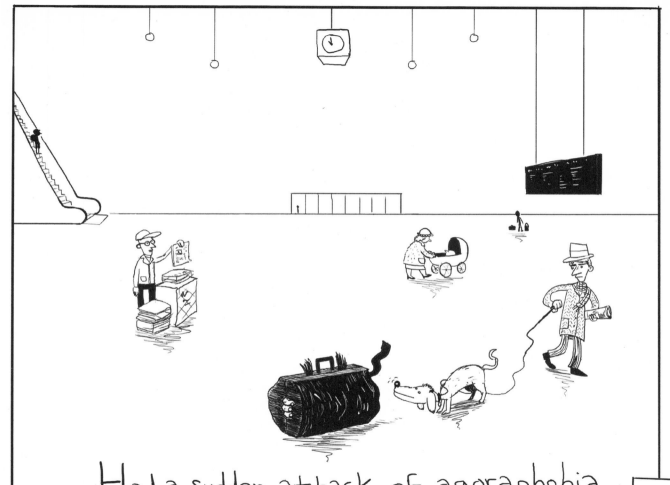

Had a sudden attack of agoraphobia

81

Decided to try every coffee place on the way to work

Discovered I'm the star of a reality tv show

83

84

Waylaid by a caricaturist

Shouldn't have worn my bread hat

85

86

Parking dispute got out of hand

Accidentally launched escape pod

87

Failed to prepare for global warming

Left the cloning machine on all night

89

Discovered my wife is having an affair

Had to call out a mechanic

Stumbled through a series of time portals

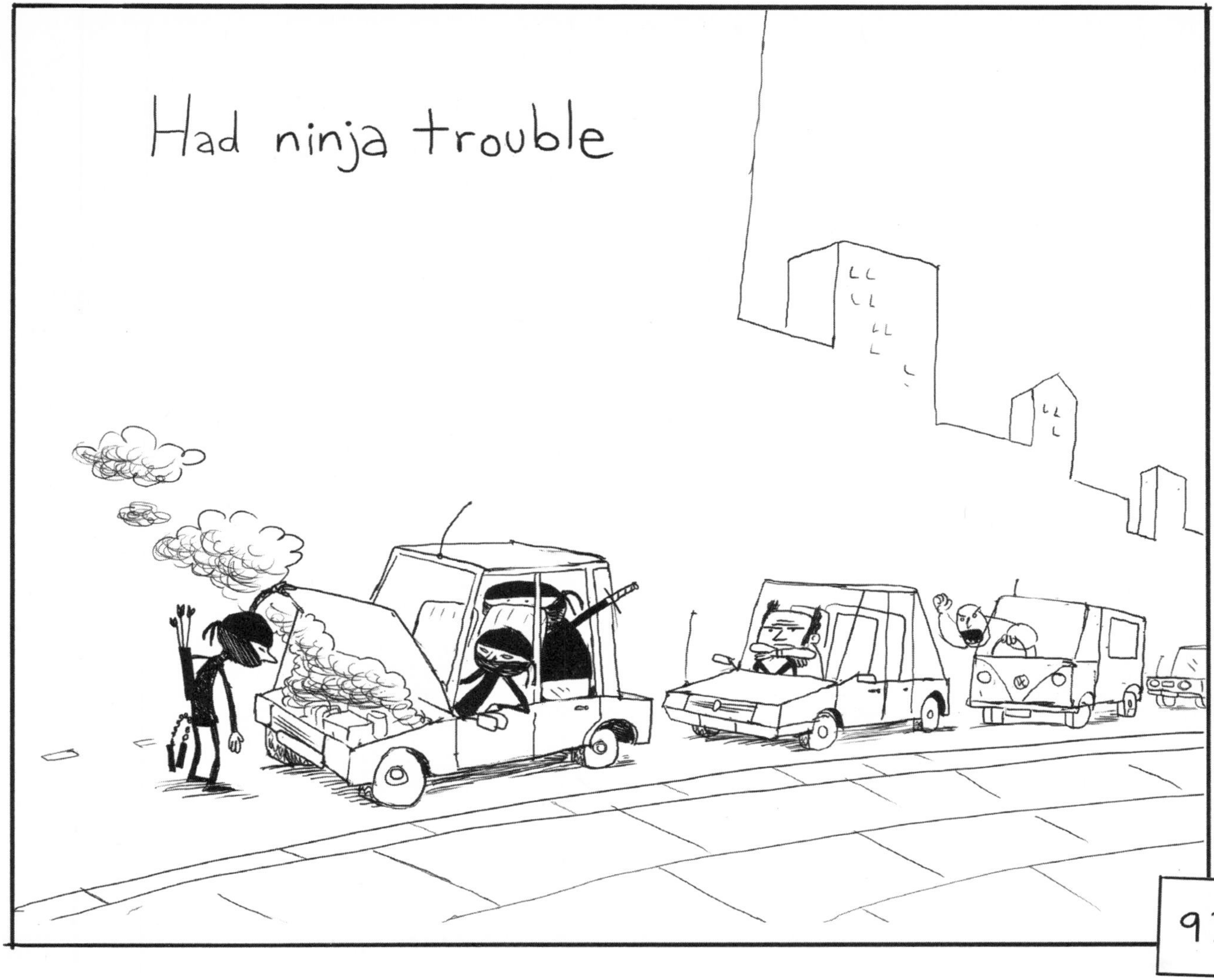
Had ninja trouble

94

Team building weekend lasted longer than expected

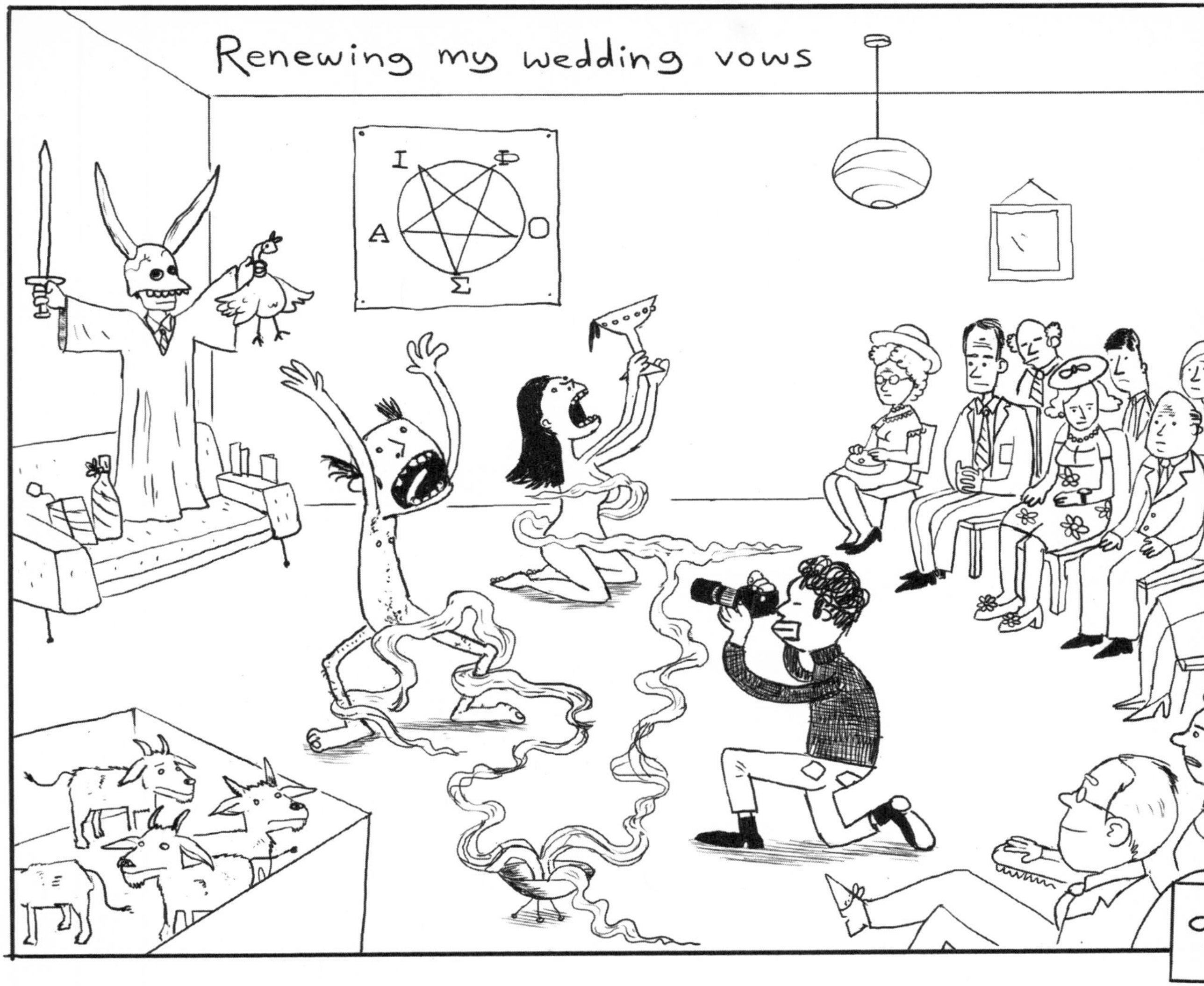
Renewing my wedding vows
I
Φ
A
O
Σ

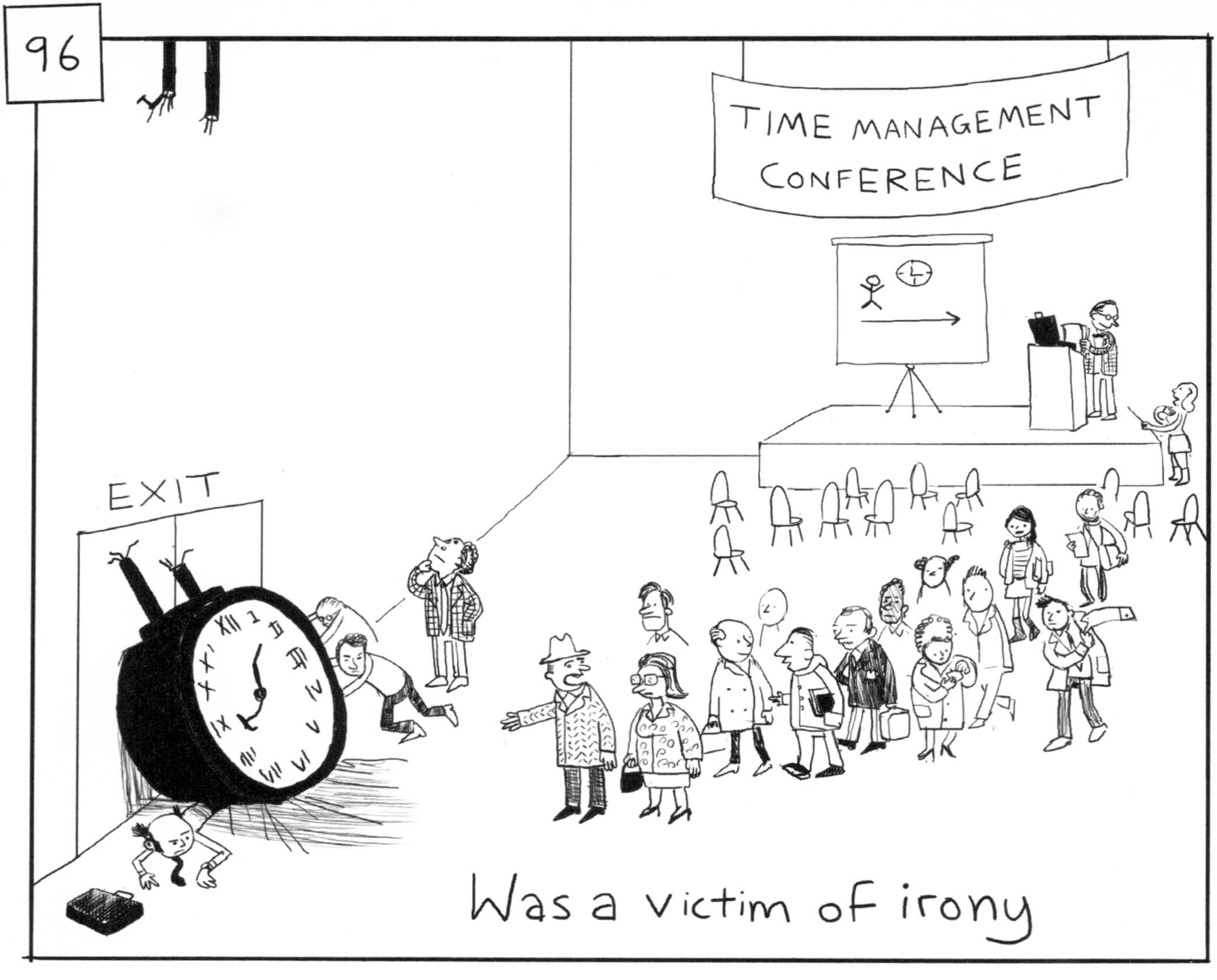
96
TIME MANAGEMENT CONFERENCE
EXIT
Was a victim of irony

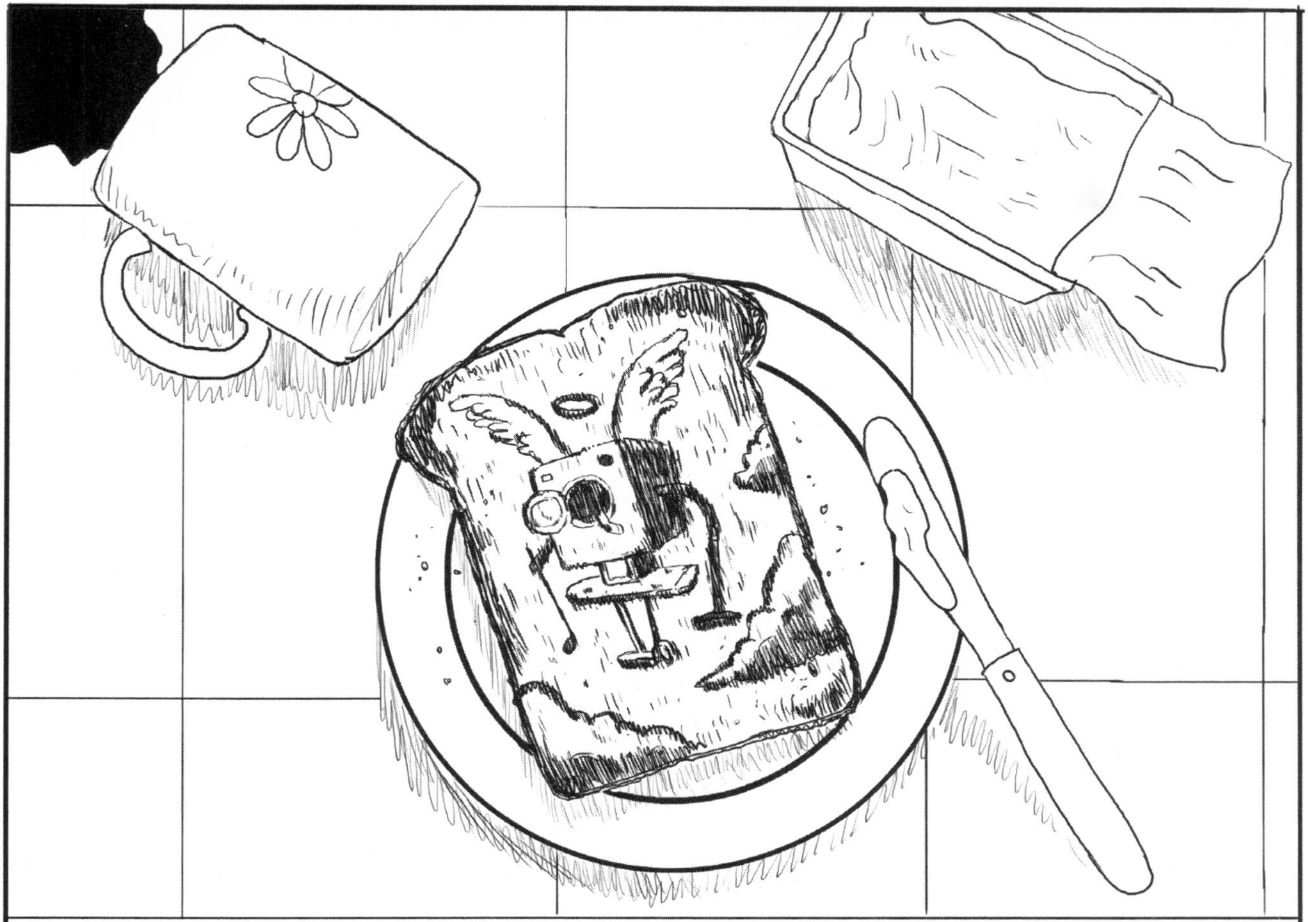

Witnessed a miracle

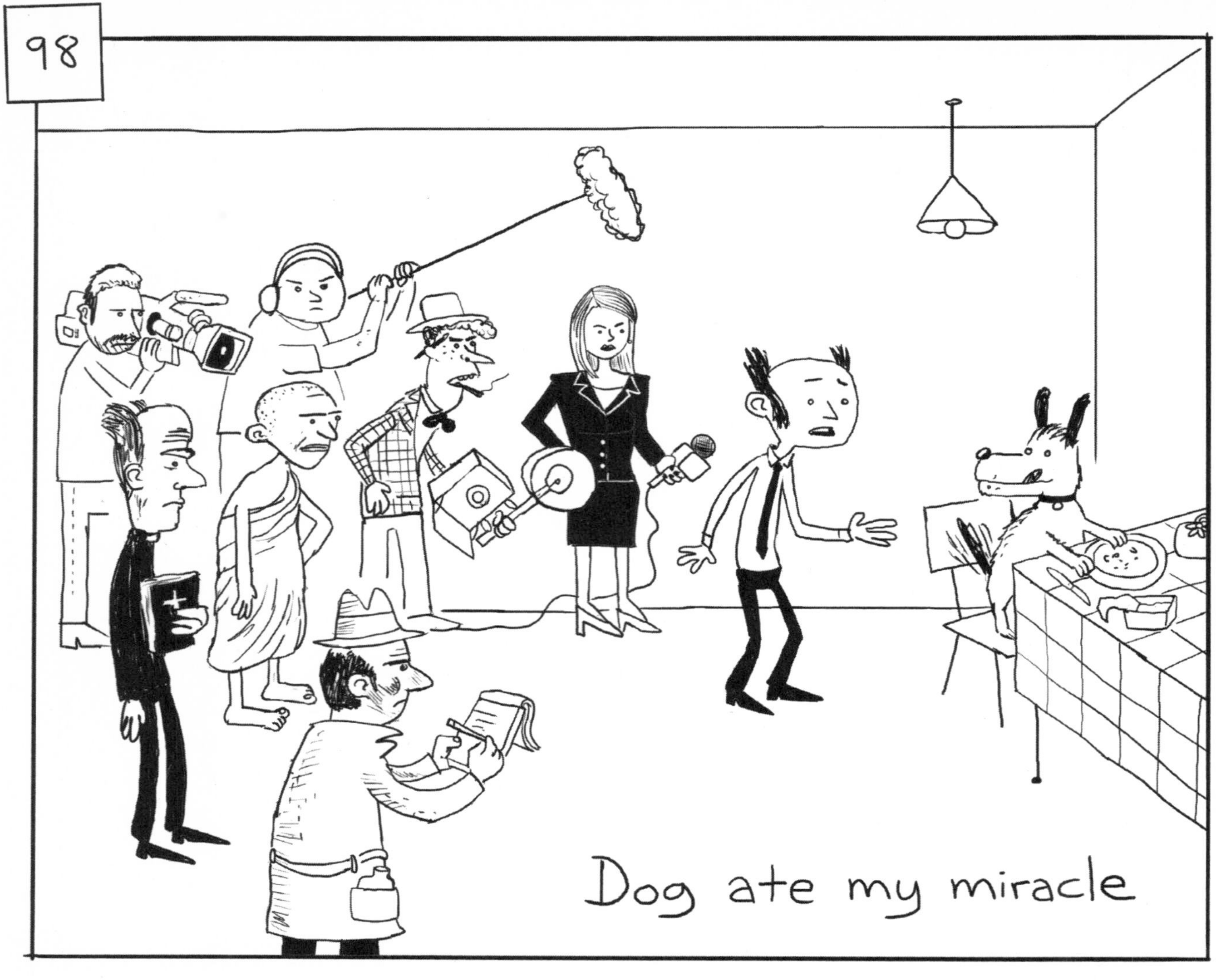
98

Dog ate my miracle

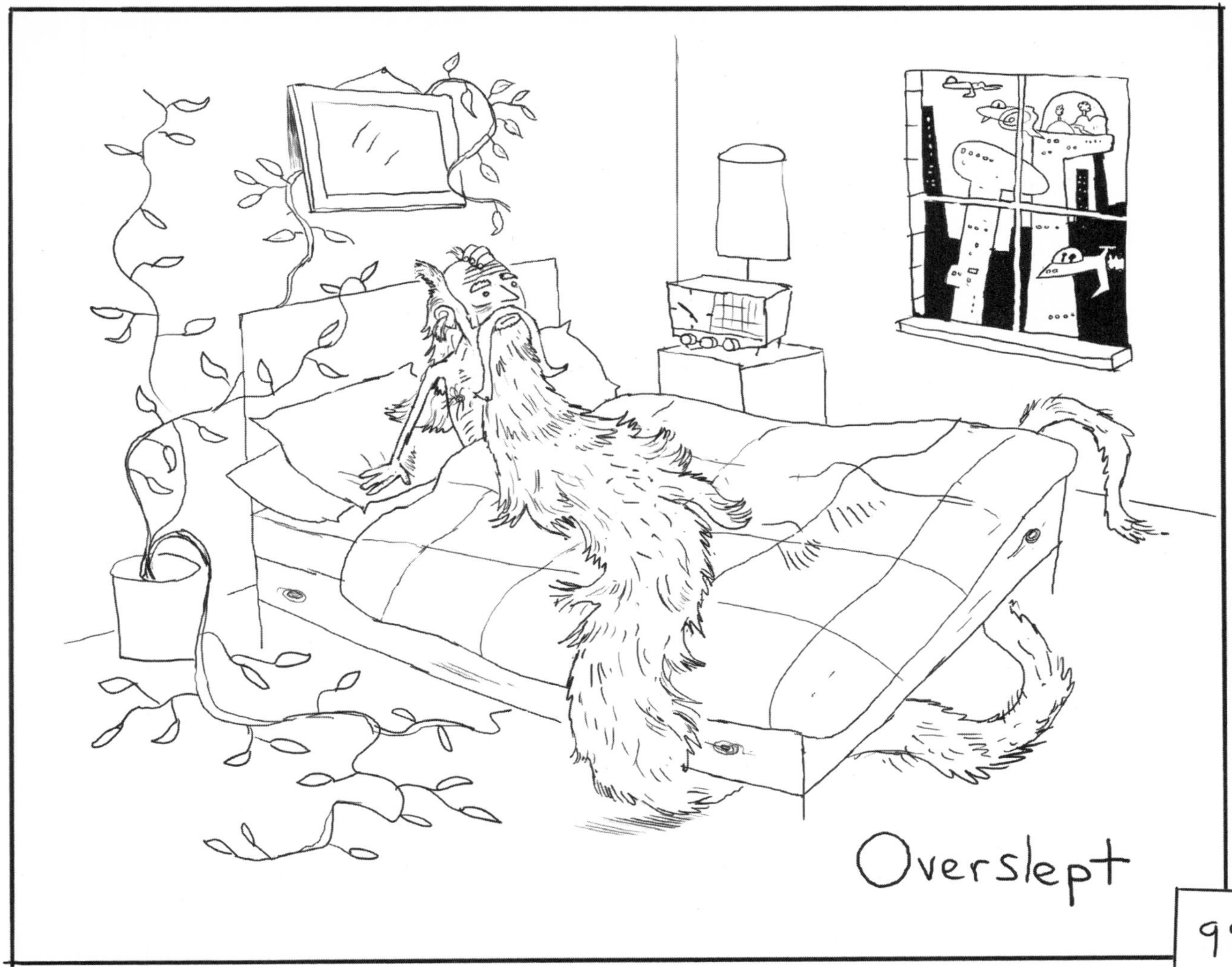
Overslept

Realised lateness is a relative concept

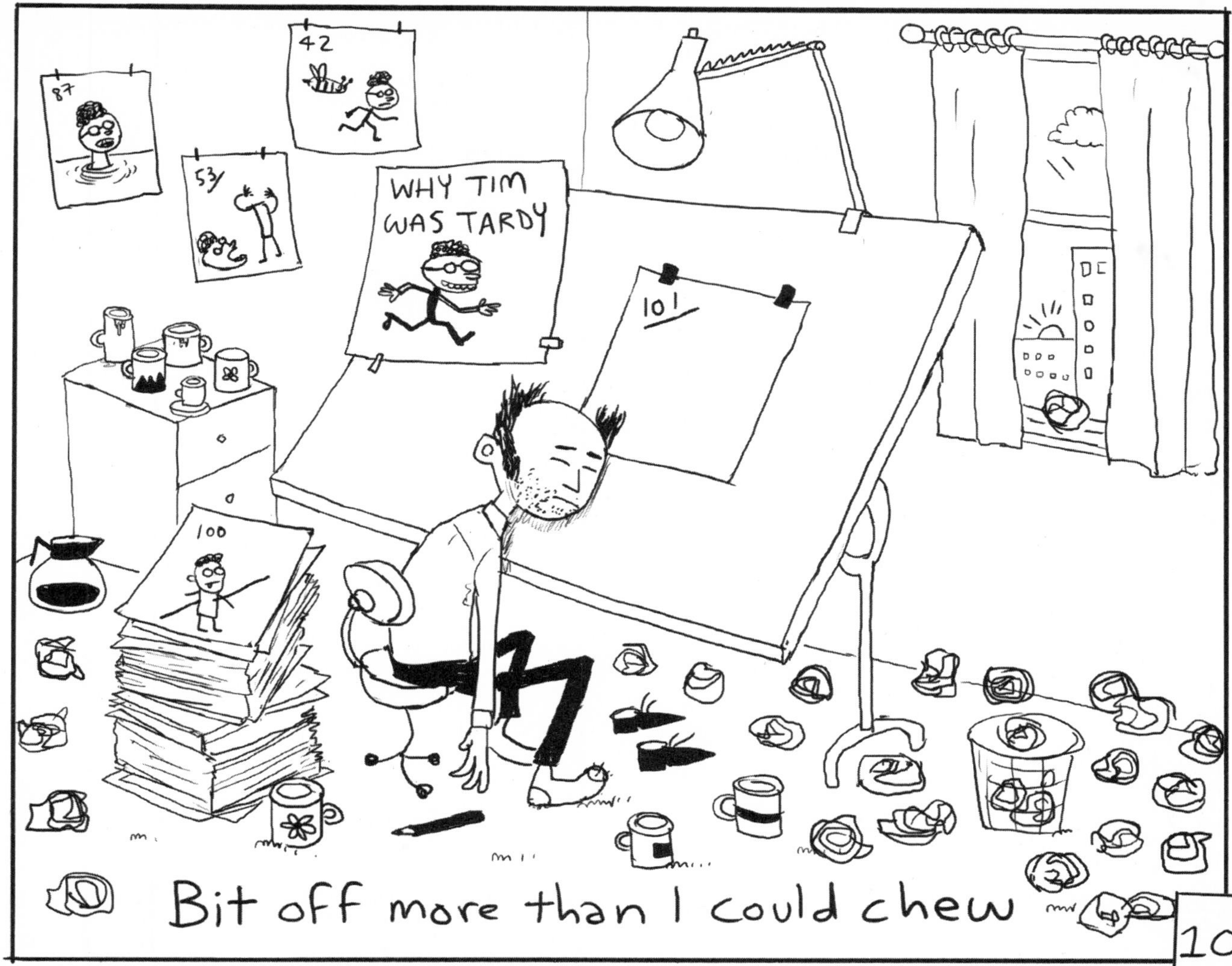
87
42
53
WHY TIM WAS TARDY
101
100
Bit off more than I could chew
101